DIGITIZING AUDIOVISUAL
AND
NONPRINT MATERIALS

DIGITIZING AUDIOVISUAL AND NONPRINT MATERIALS

The Innovative Librarian's Guide

Scott Piepenburg

INNOVATIVE LIBRARIAN'S GUIDE

 LIBRARIES
UNLIMITED™
An Imprint of ABC-CLIO, LLC
Santa Barbara, California • Denver, Colorado

Library of Congress Cataloging-in-Publication Data

Piepenburg, Scott.
   Digitizing audiovisual and nonprint materials : the innovative librarian's guide / Scott Piepenburg.
      pages cm. — (Innovative librarian's guide)
   Includes bibliographical references and index.
      ISBN 978-1-4408-3780-7 (paperback) — ISBN 978-1-4408-3781-4 (ebook)
1. Library materials—Digitization.   2. Audio-visual materials—Digitization.   3. Nonbook materials—Digitization.   I. Title.
   Z701.3.D54P54 2015
   025.8'4—dc23   2015017442

ISBN: 978-1-4408-3780-7
EISBN: 978-1-4408-3781-4

19 18 17 16 15   1 2 3 4 5

This book is also available on the World Wide Web as an eBook.
Visit www.abc-clio.com for details.

Libraries Unlimited
An Imprint of ABC-CLIO, LLC

ABC-CLIO, LLC
130 Cremona Drive, P.O. Box 1911
Santa Barbara, California 93116-1911

This book is printed on acid-free paper ∞

Manufactured in the United States of America

Figures 5.18 through 5.44 are courtesy of www.audacity.com, Copyright © 2015 members of the Audacity development team. Except where otherwise noted, all text and images on this site are licensed under the Creative Commons Attribution License, version 3.0 (http://creative-commons.org/licenses/by/3.0/). "Audacity" is a trademark of Dominic Mazzoni.

Contents

Introduction

Walking through any library convention or exhibition, it's not hard to find firms that will either digitize books, documents, photographs, and microform from your library or sell you the equipment to do it yourself. Perhaps your library or institution is part of a consortium that has a digital archives program where, for a nominal fee, you can have items scanned, stored, metadata created, and hosted, all in a single stop. This makes sense, since this consortial arrangement allows a group of users to spread the fixed costs of hardware, software, and dedicated staff over a larger area and allows them to develop specific expertise in their areas.

Many libraries, however, have more than books and photographs that are valuable. Perhaps there is a cassette recording of a local band concert or speech, or maybe some video footage either made by the library, another entity on campus, or the local television station that was donated to the library of an historic event. Some research libraries have footage of experiments that were taped for educational and professional purposes, or perhaps the library, archive, or university has some locally produced talks or public programming that is historically and educationally useful, but is too cumbersome to use, like ¾ in. U-matic tapes, or perhaps some first-generation Betamax (or Beta) tapes; maybe you have a collection of speeches on laserdisc from a company long since gone out of business or that are not available on YouTube or other similar resources. If you search for a vendor to convert these, you will quickly find that it is a small market with few vendors.

At a recent American Library Association (ALA) conference exhibit hall, there were only two vendors that offered audio and video digitization services. On the surface, this is a bit perplexing. Right now, whole generations of film and video, along with cassette, 8-track, U-matic, laserdiscs, and other plastic, magnetic, and optically based storage formats are quickly nearing the end of their life spans. In the ideal world, a collection of VHS videotapes that were used only infrequently should have been "refreshed" at least once a year by loading it into a player or fast-winder, running it all the way to the end, and then re-winding it; this process helps to re-seat the tape pack as well as help reduce any print through from too-tightly wound tape. As a side benefit, it helps the tape to "breathe" so that the adhesives binding the layers of tape together are regularly loosened and then rewound, thereby preserving their lives. The same applies to all forms of tape, including U-matic, Beta, cassette, and 8-track. 8-track tapes, if you have any, are particularly susceptible to wear because of the way they pulled tape from the center of the spool and re-loaded it on the outside. 8-tracks are a delicate balance of tension and lubricant that is easily upset by too much heat, cold, moisture, or lack of use. It's ironic that they found their biggest use in an environment known for extreme temperatures; that of the inside of an automobile.

While rare, you may have some digital audio tapes and (DAT) and digital compact cassettes (DCC.) While both are digital, they also depend on a magnetic-based recording medium, leaving them susceptible to loss and damage over time, even with error correction. The danger is particularly severe with DCCs as they are a "lossy" format, with little extra space for error correction and redundancy. Released around the same time was the MiniDisc, a format that, like DCC, is lossy but is optically based; they had the benefit of being inside a sleeve, but again, they are not immune to age and there have been reports of discs failing over time.

Figure I.01 A digital audio tape (DAT). (www.dreamstime.com)

Figure I.02 A digital compact cassette (DCC).

Last, but not least, let us turn our attention to two disc-based formats from the 70s: the LaserDisc (developed by Pioneer and Philips, among others) and SelectaVision discs developed by RCA. While outwardly similar, they used different recording techniques; the LaserDisc was optically based, while Selecta-Vision used a needle in a groove format. Intended to be the "next step" in home entertainment, their high cost and inability for home recording led to their demise, although LaserDiscs did find a strong following in libraries and schools due to their large data storage capacity and ability to "jump" from frame to frame and freeze on a particular frame (depending on the recording method used.) These discs were popular for storing the art collections of museums, speeches, and for home use, feature-length films; their quality was far superior to what videotapes could offer even under the best of circumstances, but at a price, they were large, expensive, and one needed a good television or projector along with a fairly robust home theater system to appreciate them; because of this, they didn't catch on with the masses, although they were quite popular with the audio file set; looking at a release of Disney's *Aladdin* on VHS and its counterpart on LaserDisc, one sees there is no comparison; Disney "pushed the envelope" on LaserDiscs it released to highlight the quality of its work.

Figure I.03 A SelectaVision disc in its carrier.

Of course, one cannot forget standard cassette tapes, reel-to-reel tapes (often locally made), record albums and singles, and many "book on tape" and "book on record" that were popular in the 60s but exist no more, not even online. Perhaps the library was an "early adopter" and had things like elcassettes, or maybe some old 78s in the collection, some of which might have been used for field recordings of oral history in the days before magnetic tape. Maybe you have some old "cereal box" recordings, or recordings used to advertise products or services (who knows what libraries keep; that's what archives are often for.) Many of these items are sitting somewhere, often unknown because they were "passed over" in the retrospective conversion projects as being "too costly to do right now" and "we'll get to them later when we get the major work done." They then enter the old "Catch-22" land where nobody uses them because they don't know they exist, and they aren't cataloged because nobody uses them. Sometimes there is an old player that is sitting around that still works, or perhaps not. Maybe they are just sitting there, and to be honest, maybe they need to be weeded from the collection if there is no use for them or if they don't fit into the collection.

Before weeding these items, think of the possible uses of them if users knew that they existed. A library in the Midwest recently undertook a project to catalog an extensive collection of record albums. One of the criteria was to look for a correlation between the albums cataloged and scores that had recently been cataloged. Usage of both increased, particularly when the cataloging was done at a granular level and the library supplied a USB-equipped turntable with instructions for capturing the recordings to an iPod or other portable device.

This guide is going to focus on some of the more common audiovisual formats that libraries have collected over the last 30 or 40 years: photographs, slides, records, cassettes, videotapes, and laserdiscs. Some basic information on computer hardware and software along with finding sources to play these materials will be discussed, as will techniques for capturing, editing, storing, and making them available. While you may have a different or unique source not covered here, such as DCC or DAT, the techniques and methodologies are the same, only the sources are different. Something important to remember, like any "skill" task, your first efforts may not be polished or successful; that's fine, just don't start off with "critical" or high-value items. If your first product isn't what you want, try again, make adjustments. Computers don't care how many times you do something; if you "waste" a few discs or some storage space, so be it; making mistakes are fine, so long as you learn from them.

This guide is not intended to be "archival" in nature. It will work from multiple presumptions. The first is that the library (or archive) has the resources and desire to create a "master" or archival copy of a source. This source will be stored for posterity and research with little or no alterations to it. The main criteria here will be to store a file that is as faithful to the original and has adequate metadata to facilitate retrieval with a finding aid.

The other purpose of this document is to aid in the "clean-up" of these sources so that they can be distributed and used by the general public without the damage to the sources getting in the way. This will involve the use of specialized software, some good audio and video equipment, and some plain old-fashioned seat-of-the-pants intuition about when a resulting product is "good" or needs to be redone. Again, do not be discouraged by your first few attempts; like cataloging, your first few efforts will have errors and mistakes, but as you build your skills over time, you will see a marked improvement in the quality of your work, and, one hopes, greater usage by the library's community.

A NOTE ABOUT COPYRIGHT

This guide makes no pretense on copyright guidance. For that, you should consult your organization's legal counsel or, if you have one, your organization's copyright officer. Oftentimes, in educational institutions as well as public libraries, if an item is no longer available, the original organization will allow you to make a transformative copy for use in-house (non-networked and non-circulating) if you explain the situation to them. If they do, be certain to keep all documentation regarding these permissions. Also, if given permission to copy an item, you will need to make it clear if there are any restrictions on circulating the item, classroom use, or interlibrary loan. Depending on contractual agreements, you may need to load bibliographic information into a shared utility or catalog, but if there are restrictions on access, be certain to indicate them.

Chapter 1

Getting Started

If you are reading this book, you no doubt are thinking of doing some digitization of nonprint items. The purpose of this chapter is to help focus some ideas and concepts so that you have a better idea if this is something you want to do and some considerations and decisions to make before going any further.

WHAT YOU WILL NEED

First and foremost, do you have the physical location to embark on a digitization program? Because of the noise and nature of the work, you will need a place that is at least somewhat secluded and where music, voices, and so forth are not going to be disruptive to other workers. On the other hand, you don't want to isolate the area too much as when you are capturing a source, you can do other things elsewhere in the library; you won't need to stand and watch the computer the entire time, so you will want a place that you can "pop into" every now and then to check on the progress of your recording.

Another characteristic of your project location is electricity. You will be using computers, monitors, speakers, source equipment (**VCRs**, **turntables**, tape players, etc.) so you will need adequate electricity. Because all these items generate heat, don't forget to consider that the room will need a fairly robust climate control system. While not as critical as a computer center, you will need to make certain there is adequate **AC** service and air change; a smaller room, and even midsized rooms, can become warm very quickly with all the equipment running. Heat is the enemy of electronic equipment, so a temperate environment is important, not just for the equipment but also for your sanity. In terms of electrical service, at least two 20-amp circuits, along with line conditioners and surge suppressors and an Internet connection, will be needed. Also, you will need to have available a standard **CD/DVD** player, monitor, receiver, and speakers so that you can test the results of your work outside of the computer realm.

Something often overlooked is lighting. The ubiquitous fluorescent light is perhaps the poorest choice for the work area. While economical, they can buzz at a very annoying 60Hz, resulting in background noise that will cloud your hearing when mastering recordings. **Halogen** lighting is an excellent choice, but many areas do not permit them because of the heat they generate. General **LED** or **incandescent** lighting is good. When working with videos, be aware of the color range of the lights. **Fluorescent** lighting can be anywhere from "cool" that tends toward the white/blue end of the spectrum to "warm" lights that are more pinkish and red. The next time you go to the store, notice the lighting. Oftentimes, you will find "warm" lighting in cosmetic and clothing areas as they make the items look better on you, but bluish and lighting that tends toward the white side of the spectrum in jewelry and food areas as they highlight the vividness of the products being sold. A very good mix, if a bit unorthodox, is getting some halogen shop work lights from a local building supply store and mounting them on the walls so they shine up. If they are put on dimmers (be careful of the power requirements), the lighting can be adjusted for the task at hand. Halogens have a very nice balanced range of light but, in many applications, have been made illegal because of the heat they generate, which can be a fire risk. A mix of lighting, such as some incandescent and fluorescent lights, is also an option. Note that if you go with incandescent bulbs, they may be difficult to obtain since the government has put regulations in place to encourage a move away from them. Also, incandescent bulbs do generate heat. Remember that people working on the project will be doing a lot of screen time, so an environment where the lighting can be adjusted to ease eyestrain is important. Indirect lighting is preferred, and it should not present any glare on the screen or in your line of sight. If there is a window in the room, make certain that there is some method, either curtains or blinds, so that the incoming light can be filtered or blocked entirely to ease eyestrain and enhance the ability to accurately judge colors and images on the computer and monitor screens. Another alternative would be to have very little ambient light but more "task lighting" in the way of desk and wall lamps that can be turned on and off and redirected as necessary.

Now, where does all this go? Because of the nature of the work, the computer and speakers will need to be isolated acoustically from the source devices, particularly a turntable if you are using one. Don't forget, there will be cables running from your source devices to the computer so they can't be too far away. A solution that works well, albeit it isn't the most attractive, is basic plastic office desks from an office supply company. The plastic (well, actually a recycled resin product) has very good vibration absorption characteristics and is very durable. While not the most attractive solution, it is very functional and durable. Avoid standard gate-fold tables and metal desks; these items resonate very easily, and those vibrations can be picked up by your sources and impact the quality of your recordings; they also are not at the optimum height for efficient and tire-free working. Don't forget to allocate space for supplies, discs, workspace, and so forth. The more the better.

If using a turntable, it will need to be acoustically isolated from the **speakers** and the desk; ideally, a second desk or work surface is best; acoustic isolators under the turntable may be necessary to fully isolate the turntable from room vibrations.

If budget and space permit, consider a second computer for "overhead" work. When the "capture" computer is recording information, it is not wise to use it for any other task; some users will even disconnect it from the network to prevent any automatic software updates that could interrupt a recording. The second computer would be used for making labels, cases, documentation, and others while the capture computer is recording the source information.

Now you may be asking, "labels, cases?" This will depend on what you intend on doing with the output product. If it is an audio or video product, you may want to create an archival disc in addition to an electronic file. You may even want to go so far as to create a "commercial quality" disc for distribution or for posting/download on your website. If you go this direction, you will need to ascertain if this disc and case will have artwork from the original. If an album, a **scanner** able to accommodate 12 × 12 in. originals will be necessary (most scanners are only 9 × 15 in.), as will a color printer, although this could be an existing printer already on your network. If a scanner is not feasible, it is possible to use a digital camera to take a picture of the jacket or case and then edit it in label software although the quality of the image will suffer. If you go this route, you will need a stand to hold the jacket and case as well as a tripod mount for the camera. No matter how "steady" you are, you will not be able to get a good clean image; scanning is still preferable. If your project includes scanning photographs, then consider purchasing a scanner that can do album jackets to save money. This same scanner will also be able to do "large-form" photographs. If you decide to go the camera route, be cognizant of the lighting on the original material; direct lighting will create glare. Lighting at an angle will create a good image without glare, but if the jacket is at an angle, be certain to place the camera so it is perpendicular to the image. Do not use the flash option on the camera. Since the camera has to be directly across from the original to prevent **parallax errors**, there will be a reflection in the photographed image.

Finally, don't forget people. Ideally, someone with a knack for technology and a discerning eye and ear will be needed. They will need to be able to multitask and to know when the sound is "right" and not fake or overemphasized. Music studios have developed a strategy whereby different media are edited differently. Typically, those sources that are going to be used in a car or in a portable device are mastered and equalized differently than those for home use, just so that they sound "right" in their relevant environments. You can test this for yourself by comparing a commercial CD recording of a popular artist as opposed to the download product; each is designed for a different listening environment and is **equalized** differently. The person who does this for your project will need to put his or her personal biases aside and try and engineer and master as "neutral" a product as possible. It would be beneficial to have a "listening party" at someone's home that has a good sound system to get feedback from different people if the sound is "right." It is a very subjective process, so don't be afraid to invest the time to "train" the ears of the people working on the project. An **audiophile** in your community can be a good resource. Do not trust students or workers who "live" with their headphones or ear buds; it is not possible to get a full effect of the sound with said devices, even higher-quality ones. It is advisable to "check your hearing" every now and then; the mind "forgets" sound quickly and is easily fooled and deceived.

When estimating project time, remember that recordings have to be captured in "real time." For a generation used to **ripping** CDs and DVDs in a fraction of their playing time, this can be a major adjustment. If the album runs 40 minutes (as many popular recordings from the 70s were), then it will take 40 minutes to capture that into the computer. This number can be "cheated" a bit depending on the software you are using, but then you sacrifice sound quality because of the inertia of the stylus moving at high speed. For sound recordings, it will take approximately 45 minutes to capture a recording, then another 45 to 60 minutes to edit and burn the output product. Of course, these numbers will need to be adjusted up or down depending on the length and quality of the original recording and how many "versions" of the recording you wish to make and keep. An original recording that requires more clean-up will take longer than one that is in good condition.

WHAT TO DIGITIZE

Ultimately, you may have a large array of items you will want to digitize. Once you have your equipment purchased, you will be able to amortize those fixed costs over your project; the more items you do, the less you will spend per item. Try to start small with a few wins. If you have an extensive **cassette** collection you want to digitize, then focus on that. The basic process is the same for all sources; play the source and capture it on the computer, edit the information as necessary for quality purposes, and then output it to a storage device(s). If you can do a small demonstration project for funding agencies, then the potential of them funding your main project will be greatly enhanced. One of the most effective means is to use local-source material or of notable people and demonstrate the value of reformatting it for future generations.

> **Reminder:** When starting out, don't begin with the most valuable items. Instead, practice your technique on less critical items. Develop your technique with some less critical items. Also work with one format to begin; start simple and grow from there.

When starting out, don't start with the critical or high-value/interest items. Develop your technique with some less critical items. Rest assured that as you get into the project and become more proficient, you may consider going back and "redoing" some of the earlier items. Whether you have the time and money to do so is your decision, but ultimately, you will have to say "enough" and move on to another project or source. There is a natural tendency to always want to "re-tweak" a project, just as catalogers will often want to go back and "clean up" an older record. Again, as you develop skills you may wish to go back and do some of the more critical items, but you will need to let time and budget be your guide.

Starting out, stick with one source, preferably an audio one, such as cassettes or records; working with video adds another dimension to the project; start simple and grow from there. If you stay with a single source, you will be able to leverage the purchase of the source device over a greater number of items, perhaps deferring the purchase of another source device to a different budget year.

While hardware will be covered in greater detail in subsequent chapters, a few things need to be mentioned here. There are currently on the market dedicated source devices, such as tape decks and turntable that, in addition to the standard **RCA connector** (the ones with the pin surrounded by a metal circle), have a **USB** cable for direct connection to the computer. If you choose not to go that route and use equipment you currently have, you will need to get an RCA-to-USB converter. This device can be purchased for minimal cost at any electronics supply store or many big-box retailers. Depending on the connector you purchase, it typically can also be used for your video project. It may also be included with software you purchase to do the digitization.

A word of caution on turntables. If using a good quality turntable that is not designed to connect to a computer (no USB cables), then you will need to also get a **receive**r/head unit with a phono preamp. This takes the output of the cartridge and increases it to a level the computer can use. It will also apply the Recording Institute Association of America (**RIAA) equalization curve**, which is found on records made in the 1960s and after. This curve puts back the bass that was removed during the recording process which prevents the phono cartridge from having to follow the large groove changes in low notes. If playing very old items, such as 78 rpm records, they will not have this equalization but back then there wasn't much source sound down there anyway; if you desire, it can be "re-added" during the mastering process. A USB turntable will have the preamp and equalization curve built into the USB path.

Recently, some "all-in-one" units have appeared on the market. They look like an "old-time" record player, incorporating a turntable, cassette deck, turner, and CD burner, along with proprietary software. *Eschew these units*! While useful for simple home recordings, they do not have the quality of components or software to enable you to do a satisfactory job with your project. The same goes for speakers and headphones. These critical components are the last step in the process. Many of the "popular" mass-market **headphones** on the market distinctly color the sound; go with an established brand that has been around for a while and is dedicated to full-range audiophile headphones. The same applies to speakers. For mastering, there are some very good sub-woofer/satellite combinations; these help reduce the desk space needed but can give very good results. Of course, they will need their own power supply.

For the sake of this chapter, let's assume you choose to start with cassettes since you may have an extensive collection of them from band concerts, juried performances for fine arts people, or speeches from visiting notable persons. *Do not* start with these as your first items. They are your most critical items and may be deteriorating with age and nonuse. How to "resurrect" these items to get "one good play" out of them will be covered in the chapter on sound recordings, but for now, just put them aside.

When getting started, begin with some commercially produced tapes. Even if older, they will give you the opportunity to experiment and perfect your craft. A side benefit is that, particularly in the 70s, 80s, and 90s, commercially released cassettes were of generally marginal quality (with few audiophile—targeted releases) so you will have the opportunity to hone your skills. While you won't be able to retain and circulate them (because of copyright restrictions), they are good practice sources for the more critical items in your collection and will help you become more familiar with the editing and clean-up process.

While another chapter will look at considerations for a cassette deck, one major difference is that most of the commercial tapes will use **Dolby-B** encoding, whereas locally produced tapes typically will not (depending on how they were recorded). Take a few of the commercial sources and capture them into your software and try and "clean them up." Typically, because of the way they were mastered, they will be lacking dynamic range and frequency response. Depending on the software you are using, you may be able to replace some of the lost high and low notes, but typically you cannot replace dynamic range. Experiment for a while with different filters and enhancements to see which sounds more "natural" rather than exactly like the original. While this violates one of the basic tenets of archival procedures, you can, and will, always have the original capture that you will store unprocessed for future researchers and manipulation. You can identify a deck that has the Dolby-B circuitry since it will have the logo shown in the figure.

When selecting items to digitize, try to stay with a single format so you can become proficient in that format. Also, try to remain with the same type of content, for example, if you have a large quantity of cassettes that were made of concerts at a school, do them as a group; the skills you develop with the first few will be useful for subsequent recordings. If

Figure 1.1 The Dolby logo.

you "jump around" among different contents, you will need to be more cognizant of the peculiarities of those sources.

When starting, select some items that are fairly good quality and will have a large popularity impact. Having these previously inaccessible war horses available either streaming online or on a CD will boost interest in your program and could be important for securing funding for continuation of the project. At this point, you may wish to use an old but reliable concept, the "mix tape."

For those old enough to remember, the mix tape was a common product in the 70s and 80s before the advent of portable solid-state players for making a tape of different sources. The gamut of tapes made by people ranged from "driving down the road music" to "music for the love of my life" to "music to clean my house by." In essence, it was a locally made and personal product that spoke to a person and an event. Similarly, you could make a CD or streaming file of "great recordings of the past" that could include a speech or two, selections of music, maybe some PSAs (public service announcements) that the library or local company may have done. By this tool you will be able to generate interest and support for your project. To further borrow a page from the commercial world, once you have digitized a recording, you can "repackage" them around themes or topics, resulting in a highly marketable product. These could be along the lines of "Great holiday songs from student's performances" to "A decade's worth of commencement addresses." Remember, you are not limited to like content. If an event was videotaped, it is possible to grab just the audio portion of a project, thereby allowing you to get "extra mileage" out of a source.

When considering which items to work on, remember, to the computer, a file is a file. It will take the computer just as long to "clean up" a poor master that requires extensive changes as it does to make "tweaks" to a good file. The operator's time may be different, but the actual computer time is not significantly different. This may be a consideration when considering which projects to start with.

CHECKLIST FOR CHAPTER 1—WORKROOM

1. A somewhat secluded space where noise and music will not be bothersome to others, including patrons and staff.
2. Lighting appropriate to the task. This may be all fluorescent, incandescent, halogen, or a mix of the these. Being dimmable and selectable (if there are multiple types in the room), as well as task lighting.
3. Furniture. Something durable that can hold the equipment and does not conduct sound. Computer workstations often work well for this; avoid gate-fold tables or similar devices.

4. **HVAC.** This room will have equipment in it that generates a fair amount of heat; adequate heating and cooling along with air changes are necessary.
5. Security. Given the amount of equipment and material in the room, a secure door and lock are strongly suggested; you may even wish to have an alarm on the room. Since there will be archival materials that will be stored in the room, it should not be on the "building master" but have a separate key for security. This is the consistent standard archives practice.
6. Storage space for supplies and material; again, this should be a secure space.
7. Power. Everything in the project requires electricity; try not to overload one circuit or use power strips; they can have a detrimental effect on the product.
8. Network connection for saving files to a server.

CHECKLIST FOR CHAPTER 1—SOURCES

1. Items of local or unique interest.
2. Items that highlight the necessity or desirability of the project.
3. Crowd-pleasers. Give the people what they want and like to hear so they "feel good" about the project.
4. Consider a mix file with samples of different examples to show the scope and breadth of the project.
5. Avoid rare or fragile items for your sample; you will want to "hone" your skills before tackling them.
6. Create a "take-away" for funders so they have something to remember the project by.

Chapter 2

Hardware

For any digitization endeavor, the computer (at least one of them) will be the heart of your project. For the sake of this book, a Windows-based platform will be presumed, although if you are more skilled with Apple products and feel you can make the necessary adjustments, then do so, but remember, the instructions given here, along with some of the recommended software, are designed for a Windows platform, so proceed accordingly.

In terms of computational power, obviously more is better. The author's personal experience has been with a Windows-7 operating system with **4GB** of **RAM** and an Intel dual-core processor and a 1**TB** hard drive, and to be honest, this configuration has been adequate for audio and digital processing; of course, more RAM is always desirable as are faster processors. If you plan on doing more video files, then the mastering time (the time it takes the computer to create the files for a DVD or other output) will be increased significantly if you have a slower processor or less RAM. Just make certain that it is able to connect to the Internet and has DVD disc-burning capabilities and as many USB ports as possible. This last point is important. By the time you start connecting printers, keyboards, mouse (or a **trackball**,) speakers, external drives, source devices, and others, you will find out just how fast you will run out of ports. You may find it necessary to utilize a USB expansion product, which gives you multiple USB ports from a single one on your computer, analogous to a "strip outlet" for electric power. If you utilize one, be certain that your musical and video sources are plugged directly into the ports on your computer; expansion ports may not have enough throughput for accurate results, particularly for video files.

As to the basics, a good keyboard and mouse (or trackball) are important. For the uninitiated, a trackball is essentially a mouse "turned on its back." It was popular in some arcade games, such as Space Invaders. Some gamers prefer them, particularly if it has a scroll ring and allows multiple buttons (up to four) to be programmed for different functions. They can be costly, but they require much less desk space than a mouse and can be more accurate and faster; again, your preferences will dictate if you wish to go this route. Regarding monitors, bigger, of course, is better. The size of 23 in. is about the smallest you should go, but again, if you have access to bigger, then so much the better. Having a monitor that does high definition is a good idea; if possible, one rated for gaming is ideal. Ironically, a high-quality graphics card (typically one used for gaming) isn't as necessary since the sources you will be working with typically won't have high enough quality to take advantage of it. Some "purists" insist that **CRT**-based monitors should be used; a few years ago this would have been true, but recent technological developments have resulted in **LCD** monitors that permit accurate resolution and color balance: accurate enough to yield acceptable results for your project.

Figure 2.1 A typical trackball.

A decision you will have to make is if you will use the computer that is doing the data capture will also do the graphics. By graphics, this includes scanning any covers, jackets, labels, inserts, and others and manipulating them for the appropriate storage medium, and then outputting it to a printer. Remember, while capturing data, it is inadvisable to be doing anything else with the computer, including anything on the Internet or your local network. Some advocate even completely disconnecting from the network and/or Internet because a sudden update by the antivirus, **OS**, or other software could result in the capture program crashing. On the capture computer, when doing data captures, turn off all screen and power savers. Even when recording, the computer may not think there is any activity and go into sleep mode, aborting any work you may have done.

If scanning jackets and the like for albums or discs, a large-format flatbed scanner will be necessary as jackets are typically 12 × 12 in. Of course, if you are going to output graphics for storage sources, you will need a color printer of sufficiently good quality to generate long-lasting images. Remember, you will lose a lot of detail going from a 12 × 12 in. source to a 4 ¾ × 4 ¾ in. case which is the standard size of a CD/DVD case. If you only intend to scan the artwork for posting on a website, then a good black and white printer may be adequate for your needs.

Something frequently overlooked is a good set of speakers. Yes, speakers. Most headphones or ear buds do not give an accurate sense of sound as they are often designed to work with small players and will usually have some type of "enhancement" to "improve" the sound, or they are designed to be light and easy on the ears for ease of movement. If you decide to go the headphone route for some sound work, then turn to the reviews in an audiophile publication such as *Sound & Vision* to obtain reviews for balanced, full-range, dedicated audiophile headphones. The cost for a good pair can be over $300 but is worth every penny in terms of sound quality. Headphones serve a good purpose for "close-in" hearing to ascertain nuances of sound, but only if they are of good quality and the user *knows* what good sound is. Avoid noise-cancelling headphones as they can add distortion to the sound; after all, the room you are working in shouldn't *need* any noise to be canceled! If need be, seek out the advice of someone with a full-range home system and be prepared to throw away all misconceptions of what good sound is like; this is important for good project results. Don't go for looks, go for quality sound and comfort; remember, who will be seeing you with these? Their main purpose is to give you the most accurate sound reproduction possible.

Most importantly, the value of good speakers cannot be overrated. Standard computer speakers will not be adequate to the task, but again, it isn't necessary to go whole hog and use standard home speakers with a dedicated amplifier. A good solution is a set of computer-designed speakers but in three parts: two standard speakers and a bass module. Having a separate bass module (which oftentimes will also serve as an amplifier module for the other speakers) helps to isolate the lowest notes in a location away from the source. Music at even moderate levels with high bass content can be picked up by a turntable or even a cassette deck or VCR and cause resonances and speed variations that will be noticeable in final playback. One possible solution to reduce this possibility is to do the capturing with headphones but doing the mastering with the speakers. There are also high-end speakers that connect via your computer's USB port and perform their own digital-to-analog conversion for even better sound quality, but the price of these speakers can be significant and for the purposes of this project may not justify the cost. Again, seek out the skills of someone who has access to some high-end equipment and tap their expertise. Don't trust a generation raised on MP3 or other lossy sound sources; most "golden ears" are more than willing to share their expertise.

Subsequent chapters will cover the specific software for audio and video capture as well as the source units for those activities. For now though, one piece of software that is common to all formats is some type of disc-labeling software. Some companies, such as Avery, that sell disc labels also make available templates that can be used in Word and other packages. There is also a plethora of software packages that have dedicated templates, formatting tools, artwork, and others. Some packages, after you enter the information regarding artist, title, timings, publication date, selections, format the data in the respective areas for case and labels. Some packages are free, while more sophisticated packages can be purchased for $29 to $59. Download a trial version first to see which you prefer. A personal favorite of mine is *Audio Label* (http://www.audiolabel.com/?reg). It is a very powerful and easy to use piece of software that helps format labels and case materials professionally and easily; it is also compatible with the LightScribe disc labeling product so if your drive is so equipped, it can save a lot of time and effort making disc labels. Remember to save any labels you create with the audio or video files.

Now would be a good time to go over some operational procedures. When capturing files, as soon as the file is captured, *save it*! Do this before doing anything else. For performance reasons, it is best to save the "working" file to a folder on the computer's hard drive. To simplify the process, you may wish to use some naming convention like "musicraw" or "videoraw" giving the file a mnemonic name. If doing audio files, perhaps use the last name of the performer followed by the first word or two of the title. What you use isn't important, but what *is* important is that you save the file immediately in a folder where you know where it is and you can work with it. After saving the file and performing any edits on it and then saving it to an output form (including a CD or DVD), the raw file along with the edited file(s) should be moved to a long-term storage device. This may be a network server somewhere (a particularly good option if the server is backed up regularly) or an external hard drive or sold-state device. Again, use some type of naming convention that will be easy to remember; create a folder for each "product" and put all the files in that folder along with any attendant labels, documentation, raw scan files. Audio files do not take up a significant amount of space; video files will take up more. What is important is that you save the *raw* files that were the initial capture along with any scanned materials along with the finalized output files; this way, if need be, it will be possible for others, or if the finished product needs to be reworked, to go back to the original capture file and edit it from the beginning. Researchers will also want to have access to these raw files.

> When using one computer to capture or master files, do not use it for any other task at the same time.

If you have two computers, one computer can be capturing the source material while you are preparing labels and other material with the second computer. If you go this route, be certain that the second computer is acoustically isolated from the source generator; even being on the same desk and typing can be picked up and transmitted to your output file. If you have a single computer, it is best to do all the capture and edit work, then saving the finished product *before* starting on the physical processing. Because of the demands on the computer, it is *never* a good idea to work on anything when capturing or mastering files, particularly video files.

When making any type of labels, be mindful that others may need to work with them, particularly your cataloging staff when they create the metadata for the product. Try to be "faithful" to the original source when creating labels and cases. If doing sound recordings, scanning the original source and making it available to others in the library will be a boon to their work. The same applies to video sources; scan tape labels, cases, and others even if you do not intend to use them; the information they contain is invaluable to others downstream.

This chapter has attempted to cover some of the computer hardware and software issues that will need to be addressed before you begin your project. Some, like label-making software, may not be necessary, depending on your project, or you may wish to purchase them later after your "demonstration" phase. A consideration is if you choose not to use label-making software and write directly on the disc. Be aware that some feel that the chemicals in the marker ink could damage the substrate in the disc surface as may adhesives in disc labels. Short term, it may be possible to borrow a scanner from another department or use a digital camera to capture artwork. Remember, if you go the latter route, you will need something to hold the original, a tripod mount for the camera, and suitable lighting; the results may be acceptable, but not as good as could be obtained with dedicated task-based equipment and facilities. Again, this makeshift setup may be adequate to "get your feet wet" or to demonstrate the viability of the project to your funding agency, but ultimately, you will want a more professional and dedicated installation.

In the next chapter, we will specifically look at some of the audio/video equipment you will need for this project. We will start with audio files/sound recordings as they are less complex and the equipment a bit simpler to work with; in the subsequent chapter we will look at video sources and processes.

CHECKLIST FOR CHAPTER 2—HARDWARE

1. Computer with as much processor and RAM as possible. This computer will be the "capture" computer so the more power the better. Must have CD/DVD burner drive.
2. Good-quality headphones and speakers for mastering and sound evaluation.
3. High-resolution monitor; 23 in. or larger is preferable. LCD is acceptable.
4. Line conditioner/uninterruptable power supply (**UPS**).
5. USB extension slots (if needed).
6. Keyboard and mouse/trackball.
7. Connecting cables/power cord.
8. External storage device.
9. Labeling software.
10. Disc-burning software.
11. Scanner (if capturing jackets or images).
12. Internet connectivity.

Chapter 3

Digitizing Images

Digitizing pictures, or images, requires the most basic of digitization skills and processes, processes that will be utilized in other formats, so it is a good place to start.

For equipment, a scanner with at least 1,200 **dpi** (dots per inch) is the best place to start. This means you will be looking at something beyond what you may purchase at your local big-box store. Going to a specialized vendor may be necessary. If you are not certain whether the project is going to be viable, then starting with a small inexpensive scanner as a "proof of concept" may be beneficial to convince your funding agency that the proposed project is viable.

At this level of a project, dedicated scanning and manipulation software may be included with the scanner. Frequently, these products include a color chart that can be scanned and then held up to the monitor to verify the accuracy of the scan. This is important since the master image should be as close as possible to the original source prior to editing. Depending on the scanner, it may be necessary to apply some color correction or balance prior to saving the master image.

One common error that many first-time project staff make is going with an "overly sharp" image. This is akin to sharpness on a television; using a sharpness that is too high will create an unnatural and false image that is not indicative of the original; if you wish to "sharpen" the image, that can be done with a display or edited image, it should not be done with the master image. It may seem counterintuitive that "too sharp" can be a bad thing, but an image that is too sharp does not look natural to the eye; it is an example of where too much of a good thing actually results in a poor end product.

After connecting the scanner and installing the software, you will need to go through a set of diagnostics to obtain the appropriate color balance. Typically, this will require scanning the color sample, saving the image, and then holding it up to the screen to verify the accuracy of the image. It may be necessary to adjust the scanner software to get a "true" image, and you may even need to check the image with multiple monitors to ensure that there is no distortion being introduced by the monitor.

For scanning photographs, it is best to remove them from any albums they may be in and organize them into some type of logical structure; while it is possible to create "group" of photos later, organizing the information up front and creating a logical file structure will save time later and assist those who are creating the metadata for your illustrations. Depending on what you are scanning, you may want to create a folder for all the churches in a given geographic area, another for schools, another for businesses, and others. Geographical organization has the benefit in that it closely parallels to the work of many researchers; "I'm looking for information on a given place." Admittedly, it may be "I'm looking for information about churches" but oftentimes that statement is appended with "in a certain place" so geographic organization makes sense. It also conforms to the thought process behind Library of Congress Subject Headings (**LCSH**) in that "place" is often the first subdivision in the cataloging subject heading string since that is most often how people are looking for information on a specific topic.

There is much debate about the role of hand protection in the handling of photographs. Some archivists are adamant in the role of cloth gloves to protect the photographs; others are just as adamant that washing the hands with a good soap and thoroughly drying time to remove excess dirt and skin oil is preferable. This writer tends to come down on the side of the "clean hands, no gloves" camp since it improves tactile agility and can help prevent damage to photographs when picking them up and handling them. For handling images, try to avoid metal-tipped instruments. Plastic will be less likely (but still able) to scratch photographs and images. If necessary clean photographs with compressed air and/or a soft brush. *Do not* "rub" the picture to clean it; you run the risk of scratching it with dirt on the surface. Another tendency to avoid is to "blow" on the image with your breath to clean it; avoid this. Blowing on an image will increase the moisture on it, possibly causing staining and condensation. Dusting the image with a soft brush is the best way to clean the picture if necessary.

When scanning, it is typically necessary to place the image face down. While it may be possible to scan multiple images at one time, try to resist this and scan only one photograph or image at a time. This will result in a smaller file size and simplify the creation and editing of the descriptive metadata. Make certain to keep a log of the scanned image, where it was stored, and a brief description of the image contents; again, this will aid the **metadata** staff when creating descriptive metadata for the image. When scanning, be certain to capture the border information; this could include the processing date of the photograph along with type of camera. If appropriate, scan the back of the photograph if it also contains information.

Photographs fade or color-shift over time. Even for black-and-white images, it's best to scan them on color settings. Scan and save the original image as it exists; correct for color accuracy later. For similar reasons, avoid zooming in to scan.

One question that comes up is how to handle photographs that have discolored over time. This may include fading or "color shifting" toward more **sepia** tones. Photographs that were "self-developing" such as Kodak or Polaroid instant images may have less stable color images. At this stage of the game, it is best to save the master image as is and edit later for color correction and balance. Remember, the master image is what researchers will be working with in the future, but the "public" images are what people will most likely "remember" and be interested in; having both will help drive traffic to your site which is almost always a good thing. If scanning "black-and-white" images, consider *not* setting the scanner/software to black and white. Over time, black-and-white images may experience pigment shifts or instability giving them a sepia or other hue. Again, scan and save the original image as it exists; correct for color accuracy later.

Most scanners can accommodate images up to 8 ½ × 15 in. For larger images, you will need to decide the best way to go. There are several possibilities. First, you may wish to break the image up into smaller scans and "recombine" them via the software. This will require some skillful editing and may result in cumbersome and less-than-useful images. Another option is to send those items out to a vendor that has the necessary dedicated equipment. Be prepared for a high per-item cost rate. A third option, depending on the size of the item, may be to take a "picture" of it with a digital camera. While it allows for capture of the entire image, resolution and quality will be sacrificed. It also requires the creation of a special location with appropriate balanced lighting to capture the image. Flash lighting is not acceptable as this can cause "hot spots" in the final image. A possibility is to take a "master" establishing shot of the entire subject and then smaller, more detailed captures of individual areas. At this point, it may be necessary to consult with local photography experts as to camera, lighting, and the like. If using a camera, select one that will allow to take the image without digital zoom; digital zoom only makes the individual pixels larger, thereby compromising image quality. Ideally, try to avoid any type of zoom, particularly digital, but optical can also introduce distortion. This will preserve as much of the original image quality as possible. Again, it may be necessary to image-correct using software so that the captured image is as close as possible to the original.

For some projects, you may also have the negatives available, or perhaps *only* have the negatives. When scanning these, again, scan them "as is" but try not to apply any correction to them. Some scanning software has a "negative" feature that allows it to recognize the scanned image as a negative and adjust color and balance accordingly. A useful feature of many software packages is that they allow for the creation of "positive" images based on the negatives. When saving files, be certain to save a master file as well as a "positive" image of the negative; also, develop a naming convention that assures the negative is saved with the same type of file name/descriptor as the positive image to facilitate retrieval. With negatives, they may be on a strip; it may be advisable to save the strip as a whole unit while also saving the individual images off the strip with their matching scanned positive images. Under *no* circumstance should images in a strip or on a "wheel" be cut apart; this can result in negative damage and increases the risk of them being lost.

When saving files, the preferred formats are **.TIFF** or **.JPEG**. TIFF is preferable in that it is a lossless format and can be used to combine multiple images into a single file. While .JPEG is very common, it has the potential to be "lossy" and should be avoided. The suggested file structures permit a high degree of accuracy when editing and portability and can be "manipulated" by many software editing packages.

CHECKLIST FOR CHAPTER 3—DIGITIZING IMAGES

1. Use a scanner of at least 1,200 dpi with a screen size able to accommodate the larger images in your collection.
2. Install the editing software and perform any color balancing.
3. When scanning images, save the image "as is" for a master image.
4. Do not use the "black and white" scan option for black-and-white images; they can be corrected later; "black-and-white" images may not be truly "black and white."
5. Devise a file storage convention to simplify organization and metadata creation. Some type of structure that is by subject of the photograph along with a place is a good option.
6. Do not cut apart any negatives; scan as a single unit for the master file; they can be broken apart for the "display" images.

Chapter 4

Digitizing Slides

Many libraries have an extensive collection of photographs and other similar resources. The previous chapter looked at the scanning of images such as photographs. This chapter will look at the process of digitizing slides since they can be a bit more problematic.

At first it would seem fairly simple. Just place some slide face-down on a scanner bed, crank up the resolution, and scan away. The problem with this method is that the image is being lit from the *front* as opposed to the *back* as slides were designed to be shown. We are going to look at some methods of digitizing slides and the relative merits of each.

The first such option is what is called *slide-to-photo*. In this arrangement, the slides are loaded into a projector with the images shown on a screen placed one to two feet from the projector. The camera is placed as close as possible to the projector, and a "picture" is taken of the screen image. The good part of this is that it is relatively cheap. Unfortunately, that is about the only thing it has to go for it. Because it is impossible to place the camera and projected image in direct line to each other, there will be an inevitable amount of **keystoning** in the final image. Also, the image will only be as good as the light source and lens in the projector. Unless you have upgraded either or both, the resulting product will certainly not be of archival quality. Some companies tried doing this with **16 mm** films when video became popular; they would point a video camera at the screen and "film" the movie. While inexpensive, the defects in the original were quite obvious and the picture quality was poor, generally limited to the darkness of the room, the light output of the projector, and the reflective quality of the screen.

The next step-up from this is to get a specially designed *mirror box* for a flatbed scanner. This device routes a significant amount of light *around* the back of the slide, creating a more natural effect. The operative word here is "significant" as a large volume of light still is coming from the front of the slide. Any specks of dust will be noticeable in your finished item, but again, the cost is relatively small. This may be an option if you are doing a very limited number of slides. Note that the mirror box is unique to the particular scanner you are using so you probably will not be able to use any old scanner you have around for the project in favor of a more high-end scanner/mirror box arrangement.

A more cost-effective option, if you are doing a small amount of slides, is an inexpensive slide converter. These come in various types and styles, but for the most part, you load the slides into them and they are converted to a digital form.

Figure 4.1 A slide converter.

Prices run from just over $100 (although reviews for these have generally been negative) to some that are over $1,400. You will need to make the decision as to what level of quality you desire, the volume of slides you have, and the condition of the slides as well as the funding you have. If you have a small quality, then a less-expensive product may be adequate. If you have a large volume of slides, then a more powerful device with more features may be called for. As with all things, there are tradeoffs on price versus quality and convenience.

A method many photographers consider the best is a slide holder that mounts directly to a **35 mm** camera. This has the benefit of creating a "closed" environment between the slide and the camera lens as well as being in a direct line. A side benefit is that when taking the picture, the resulting image will already be in a digital format to simplify editing. If you go this route, be prepared to invest in a dedicated camera and slide holder apparatus. Depending on the quality of the tools you use, this can become a very expensive proposition. Also, you will need to consider how the camera stores the images. Obviously, film is out of the question, and CDs can become cumbersome. The best option here is a flash drive that can be interfaced directly to your editing computer. After moving the files from the camera to the computer, *immediately* save them to your long-term archive storage location (network, external hard drive, etc.) so that you will not risk losing the original image if you subsequently edit them. A drawback of this process is that slides have to be done one at a time and there may be some "**cropping**" issues with the slide and camera, resulting in the very least a white boarder around your slides or losing some of the image; neither possibility is very desirable.

Another option some have used with good success is a dedicated camera-plus-slide holder. These dedicated devices have a slide holder, light source, and camera built into a single unit. The benefit of these is that they are typically designed from the ground-up as a unit, allowing the entire unit to be "tuned" to work as one, thereby having the potential to improve quality.

Yes, that paragraph had a lot of qualifiers. Some units sell for as little as $80 at your local department store and can run into several hundred dollars at a good photo store. As with all other digitization tools, the first-level conversion place is *not* the place to cut corners. If the initial image is bad, then you will either have a poor-quality final product, or spend an inordinate amount of time "cleaning up" the image. If you choose to go this route, be prepared for a significant "upfront" investment. Most units will connect to your computer via a USB interface. A downside with many of these units is that slides have to be handled one at a time or in groups of five, which can be cumbersome and time-consuming.

When considering a scanning source, look for one with *at least* 1,200 dpi (dots per inch); 2,000 dpi is better. Again, the initial upfront costs will be higher, but the resulting product will be better. A tool that can be very useful is a light table and viewing lens. This will help you see better the "natural" color of your original source so that any corrections can be accurate, even if it means making the scanned image "wrong" so that it matches the original.

When purchasing a scanner, some will come with dedicated software. Normally, this is not unusual in that it often drives the scanner, serves as an interface between the scanner and your computer, and offers a way to manipulate the scanned images. Be careful of any software that comes with a scanner; it may be programmed to "normalize" the scanned image so that it looks "correct." While desirable for home use, for archival use this can be disastrous. This is not to say that all "correction" is bad. Depending on the hardware and software used, the designer may "know" that certain colors and images are not scanned accurately so the software "fixes" those errors to give an accurate (at least compared to the original source) image. If the software is designed to give "natural" colors to the scanned image, then it should be deactivated. If the scanner/software cannot scan the original accurately, then look at a different product. A downside with many light-based technologies is that as a bulb ages it can experience color-shift, moving the resulting image "warmer" or "cooler" over time. Check to see if the scanning software is able to overcome and/or correct for these errors.

> Before beginning, think about a logical progression for your project.

Plan out ahead how each slide relates to the others in your collection, before starting to digitize. Ideally, all the slides you will be scanning will be present so you can organize them into logical groups. While slides are scanned one by one, knowing in advance how each digital image file relates to the others in the collection will make it so much easier to use metadata, finding aids, and/or webpage design to present the collection to your users in an organized fashion. This can help your cataloging/metadata people later as they assign descriptive terms to the images. Even if you don't have all the slides you are going to scan, it's not that critical as they can be reordered or reorganized later. Ultimately, it will be up to your finding aid and metadata tool to "bring together" related images. This is where the **light box** will help; it can aid you in organizing your slides into logical groups.

Some other valuable tools are canned air, some soft brushes, some soft cloths (non-linting, of course), and a viewing lens. These tools will help you "prep" your slides before scanning. The canned air can be used to blow dust and dirt off the slides. As with photographs, *never* blow directly on the slides with your breath. Human breath is moist and can cause condensation on the film; the water vapor can also cause discoloration of older images. If the slide mounts are cardboard, the moisture can cause delamination of the glue and potential mold and rot. The brush can be used for more stubborn specks, but never "rub" the slide, particularly if you are holding it in your hands. It is far too easy to press too hard and cause deformation of the film layer. The viewing lens looks something like a jeweler's **loupe** (only larger) and can be used to scan slides before they are mounted into your scanning device to verify there is no dust on the slide.

Figure 4.2 A slide viewer.

Note that the base of the viewer is sized to completely fit over the slide and its mount; this is to reduce spurious light from affecting the image you view.

If there are scratches on the slide, *do not* attempt to clean them out in any way; they are a part of the film and should be scanned as such. It may be possible to edit them out later, but that should not be done in your master copy.

Some slides may have experienced color distortion. If so, do not "clean it up" for the master copy. Physically clean the slide as thoroughly and safely as possible prior to scanning. After scanning, save the image as a. TIFF format as it is lossless, albeit more space intensive. Do not use. JPEG as it is a "**lossy**" format and will not serve well if the image is later enlarged electronically. One benefit of. tiff files is that multiple images can be combined into a single image. After scanning, create a basic log that documents the file name along with the location of the file and a *brief* description of the image. As an adjunct to this, you may wish to download software that allows you at a later date to view camera-generated metadata regarding the image. This can include the type of camera used, date, exposure settings, and others. This is typically called **EXIF** data, and various pieces of freeware that harvest this data can be downloaded. This same software can be used to harvest metadata for some scanned images as well as video images. An example of some of this metadata is listed here.

This will aid the metadata creator in locating and tagging the image at a later date. It will be "carried along" with the image at all times and is separate from the metadata your cataloger will create later. Another option, if you are working with the actual image, is to right-click on it, then select *Properties* and then *Details*. This will give you much the same information, if it is available.

There are many good editing tools out there. The obvious choice is Photoshop, but it can have a steep learning curve and with it you run the risk of "over-editing." The Microsoft Office photo editor is a good place to start. Learn what you can do and what you *want* to do to your images. Something that can be useful are multiple versions of an image, particularly if the original image has extensive sepia tinting to it. This is more common if the original slide was in black and white. If the slide has experienced discoloration, then save one version as your "master" version, another "**color-corrected**" to make it "natural" given the image, and consider a **falsed** black-and-white version, particularly if the original was black and white and has gone to sepia. Of course, you should make all versions readily available to researchers and fully

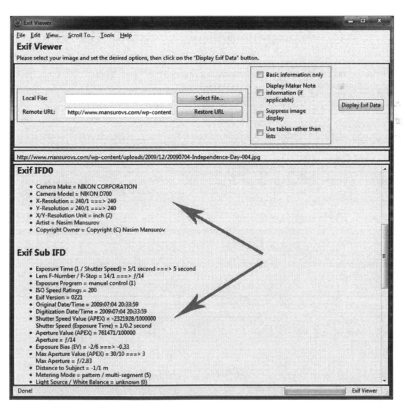

Figure 4.3 EXIF metadata.

disclose any editing you have done. If you don't like the editing that you can accomplish in Microsoft, then look at other purpose-designed packages. Many will allow for trial downloads to trial a version. Don't be afraid to ask local professionals about packages they use. Some may be exactly what you are looking for, but may be out of your price range; there are tradeoffs to what can be done and what you can afford; be aware of them and be aware that at times you may need to substitute "manpower time" for "software costs."

After scanning the slides, pack them into acid-neutral boxes, label them, and store them in a cool, dry area, with humidity around 50 percent. As has been discussed earlier, you should store your master file and any edited file on both an external drive and a network server that is regularly backed. Server backups and file rotations will be discussed in subsequent chapters.

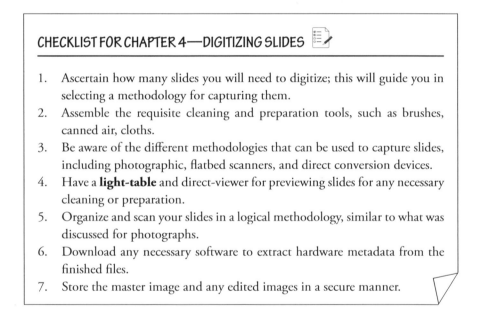

CHECKLIST FOR CHAPTER 4—DIGITIZING SLIDES

1. Ascertain how many slides you will need to digitize; this will guide you in selecting a methodology for capturing them.
2. Assemble the requisite cleaning and preparation tools, such as brushes, canned air, cloths.
3. Be aware of the different methodologies that can be used to capture slides, including photographic, flatbed scanners, and direct conversion devices.
4. Have a **light-table** and direct-viewer for previewing slides for any necessary cleaning or preparation.
5. Organize and scan your slides in a logical methodology, similar to what was discussed for photographs.
6. Download any necessary software to extract hardware metadata from the finished files.
7. Store the master image and any edited images in a secure manner.

Chapter 5

Audio Recordings

RECORD ALBUMS AND TURNTABLES

At this point let's assume that you have all your computer hardware setup, a good workspace arrangement, scanner, printer. For this chapter, we are going to look at some of the mechanics and issues of capturing sound recordings.

Why sound recordings? First, there are fewer commercially available audio recording formats than video formats. And it makes sense to begin by working with sound only. Second, with audio recordings, there is only one dimension to work with, the sound. With video sources, there is not only the sound, but also the picture; we want to build our skill set slowly and on a firm foundation; many of the concepts learned by capturing audio files will come back to serve as the starting point for capturing video files.

EQUIPMENT

Before we can determine *what* sources we are going to digitize, we will need specialized software to effect the conversion. One product that is widely used is a package called *Audacity*. One of the benefits of Audacity is that it is available as a free download; it is a shareware product that has a large following. Its major strength is that it has a wide range of file manipulation tools; you are really limited only by your imagination, time, and computer power. Another strength is that since it is so widely used, there is a large base of users out there to offer support; remember, as a shareware product this is no vendor to go to. If you feel uncomfortable with that type of situation, you may wish to consider using a commercial product with some type of support arrangement. There are many good products out there at low cost that should fit your needs, but before purchasing, make certain the package has the features you will need and the support you desire. Because of its large user base, there is a very useful Audacity wiki available to help with questions.

One downside to Audacity, and this can be major or minor depending on your viewpoint, is that it can have a steep initial learning curve, but as with most software packages, once you reach a level of basic competence, it is relatively straightforward to migrate to other audio sources depending on their characteristics. Again, don't hesitate to spend some time looking at the Audacity wiki site for guidance. To locate the site to download Audacity, just Bing "Audacity download" and select the version for your computer. There are versions for Windows and Mac, but this book will only speak to the Windows version; those who have more skill and experience and Apple products may wish to go the Mac route, but because the installed base of users is smaller, there may not be as much support for it in the wiki as the Windows version. As with all software, you should create a *download* folder on your computer's hard drive to download the file into and then scan it with your antivirus software. The author has never encountered any viruses or malware in Audacity, but it never hurts to be safe. For more guidance on downloading, installing, and configuring Audacity, see the end of this chapter. Remember that there may be updates or enhancements since this book was written. A basic working knowledge of Windows' file structure and control panel is assumed for many of the operations described here.

The next decision you will have to make is what sources you will want to digitize. For the sake of this book, we will look at two: record albums and cassette tapes as they are most common forms found in libraries. If you have other forms, such as **8-track** or **reel-to-reel** tapes, the basic process is the same. For unique sources, such as music boxes, that will require an acoustic method of transcription; we will look at those later.

Record albums (and singles) represent perhaps the largest area of a collection that a library may wish to digitize, and to that end, there are many directions a library can go. As we discussed earlier, if one chooses to use an existing turntable, then it will be necessary to find a receiver or tuner with a *phono* input and a **line-level** output (e.g., a *tape* output). This is necessary since the receiver/tuner will have the RIAA (Recording Industry Association of America) equalization curve in it; without it, your recordings will sound "bass shy" and thin. If you opt to use a USB-equipped turntable, it will have the curve built into it. Some recordings, such as old 78 **rpm** recordings, will *not* have the curve mastered into them; using a receiver/ tuner will result in the loss of some bass, but remember, given the age and possible condition of these recordings, they probably don't have any bass content anyway. One good thing about Audacity is that it has the ability to add bass back into a recording based on the settings; more on this later. If the turntable you have access to only has speeds of 33⅓ rpm and 45 rpm, never fear. Again, Audacity has a way to take a recording played at 33⅓ and convert it to the equivalent 78 rpm recording. If you have some of these recordings, check with the manufacturer of the turntable/head shell to find out if a specialized stylus will be necessary. The Audio-Technica turntable shown here (fig 5.1) has received many positive reviews as a good product at a good price (around $400 at the time of writing), but there are other products out there for less money (with correspondingly less good performance), but they may be good for the "demonstration" phase of your project.

What's a **head shell**? In audio terminology, it's the part at the end of the tone arm that holds the **cartridge**. The cartridge is the assembly that holds the **stylus** (or needle) and converts the lateral grooves on the record into electrical energy for the stereo receiver or

Figure 5.1 Audio-Technica AT-LP120-USB turntable. (cdn.kaskus.com)

tuner. In modern turntables, it is not uncommon to purchase the cartridge (the assembly where the stylus is held) separate from the turntable. This is so users can spend as little or as much as they want, depending on the quality of sound they desire, the condition of their records, and the particular geometry of the turntable; some cartridges work better with certain turntables than others, and some cartridges are designed for more rigorous use (as in **DJ** or radio station environments) than in home use. Again, consult with a reputable dealer for guidance on this topic. A typical head shell is shown here. Some turntable manufacturers specify a certain type, depending on if it is a straight or curved tone arm. Again, check with a specialized source for guidance.

As alluded to earlier, if one uses an existing turntable, then it will need to be connected to an outboard receiver/tuner. One function of these devices, as already stated, is to apply the RIAA equalization curve. Another function is to boost the signal level coming from the cartridge to a level other

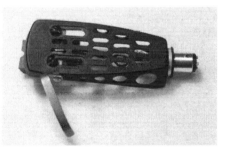

Figure 5.2 A standard headshell.

sources can use. If you were take an adapter and connect a standard turntable directly to your computer, you would hear little, if any sound; the signal level is just too low for the computer to work with. Using an external amplifier allows the signal to be "boosted" to a level the computer can work with. If using a receiver/tuner, you will need to get an RCA-to-USB adapter. This device will usually have three male RCA connectors on the end and a male USB connector on the other. As covered in Chapter 1, RCA connectors are the ones that you are used to seeing on most audio and video equipment. It has a post in the center with some shielding around the outside; they are available at just about any electronics store and at some larger department

Figure 5.3 Phono inputs on the back of a receiver.

stores. Again, if you are using a turntable with a dedicated USB connector, this will not be an issue. If connecting a turntable to the back of a receiver, make certain to connect it to the *phono* inputs, *not* the *tape* inputs; you would have distorted sound. The phono inputs are circled on figure 5.3.

Why three connectors though if we are only doing stereo? Ultimately, we are also going to want to do video, so the third connector will be for video. Typically, these three connectors are going to be of three different colors: *red* for *right*, *white* for *left*, and *yellow* for *video*. While there may be some variations (e.g., instead of white the connector may be black), most cables

Figure 5.4 A standard RCA connector.

Figure 5.5 A USB connector.

adhere to this scheme. If you are going to be doing video sources also, it would pay to look at the source you will be using. VCRs will typically only have an RCA or **coax** (standard TV cable) connector; some newer units may use an S-connector, which sort of looks like a round plug with five pins inside of it. **Laserdisc** players will usually have both; as a general rule, an **S-connector** is going to give you a better image, but depending on your source material and the unit you are recording from, it may not be worth the extra cost.

Here are some pictures of the different connectors that we have discussed.

This is a standard RCA connector. While there are variations on the plug, they generally have a center pin with a metal shield around it. This is a *male* RCA connector. The receptacles on most equipment are *female* connectors.

This is the standard USB connector. They are found on most modern computers and for the purposes of this book, on some dedicated turntables and cassette decks.

This is an S-Video connector that you may find on some late-model VCRs and laserdisc players. If given the option, this is a better method to take video from your source as it has more channels to carry information and can result in better picture quality.

Figure 5.6 An S-Video connector.

This is an RCA-to-USB converter. It has three female RCA connectors. The red lead is typically for the right audio channel (just remember "red for right"), the white lead is for the left audio channel, and the yellow lead is for video. Notice that it also has an S-Video connector. All the leads on this device are female, which means you will need a male-to-male cable

Figure 5.7 An RCA-to-USB converter.

to connect it to the output device; these male-to-male leads are readily available at just about any electronic and larger department stores. There are some "high-end" cables that purport to improve sound/picture quality and can be very expensive, but for our purposes, the supposed benefits do not outweigh their cost.

There are also after-market "**head amplifiers**" available. These small boxes are simple amplifiers that a turntable plugs into and has either USB or RCA connector outputs. The head unit cuts down on the equipment needed and provides the necessary equalization and amplification of a turntable's output so that it can be used by a

Figure 5.8 A head amplifier. (images. junostatic.com)

computer. If a good quality receiver/tuner is not available, then this may be the way to go.

The connections on this are pretty basic. Two leads run from the turntable into the input side (on this box, on the left) and then two leads run from the output (on the right) to the receiver. Note that this will require a power source.

When you have a turntable and receiver/tuner, you are ready to start making the connections. You may be asking, "what is the difference between a *receiver* and a *tuner*? In audio parlance, a receiver is a device that you plug various sources into, be it a turntable, cassette deck, CD player, DVD player, or other source. It has tone, volume, and source selection tools to allow the user to select what source they want to utilize, how loud they want it, any tone adjustments or other ways to modify the sound, then generate an output signal strong enough for speakers to play the material. A *tuner* is similar to a receiver except that it has no amplifier to generate the power necessary to drive speakers. This book is not going to get into the merits of one over the other (and rest assured, audiophiles become quite vehement in arguing the merits of one over the other) suffice to say that whichever unit you have will work fine. Just connect the turntable to the *phono in* connections and your RCA-to-USB converter to an output option, typically one of the *tape* outputs. Remember, the turntable is connected to the *input,* and the adapter is connected to the *output.* It is important that the turntable is connected to the phono connection as it has the special amplifier in it to boost the signal to a level that can be used. If you are using a dedicated head amplifier, then simply connect the turntable to the input and your adapter to the output area. There, good to go. The tone controls on the receiver/tuner will not make any difference as sound going from an input to another line-level output is typically not processed; the volume/tonal processing occurs only when the signal is passed to the final amplifier stage or the speakers. The following is the back of a typical receiver with some of the aforementioned connections circled.

Note that in the example shown we are using the *tape* out. This particular unit calls it *recorder,* but the function is the same. A good way to remember

Figure 5.9 Tape connectors on the back of a receiver.

the terminology is that devices that *generate* sounds are connected to the *in* connections, while those that *want* the sound are connected to the *out* connections.

One benefit of using the receiver/tuner arrangement is that if you decide to engage in other digitization projects, those sources, such as cassette deck, 8-track tape player, or reel-to-reel deck, will also connect to the unit. It is possible that a VCR or laserdisc player can be connected, but because of the capabilities of some units, it is typically better to bypass them and go directly to the computer. Some audiophiles suggest that you should get an external ADC device. ADC stands for *analog to digital converter*. It converts the analog signal coming from your source into a digital signal that can be fed into the computer. This was required for older computers, but in newer computers a good quality sound card can yield as good, if not better results, particularly if the card is designed for gaming. It is possible to get higher conversion and sampling rates with external converters, but they can be costly. If starting from the ground-up, a high-quality sound card installed in the computer can yield just as good results. The "basic" external converters, as well as most internal computer sound cards, will result in "CD quality" sound, for the intents and purposes of the projects you will be doing, this will be adequate.

These last few pages may seem very daunting, like there is a lot to do and learn, and if you have little or no background in turntables or audio systems, then it is, but even someone who is a relative novice in the area of home theater or home sound equipment should have little problem with the connections. If, however, you feel this is all very intimidating, there is another path that you may wish to consider.

The earlier scenario is predicated on the fact that you want to use existing items that you may have around your facility; this is not a bad thing, but you will need to ask yourself: "are these items of a quality that I will get an acceptable result from them?" Depending on the age and condition of the equipment, that may not be the case, particularly in the area of turntables. Turntables purchased for libraries typically were designed for durability as opposed to sound quality; many did not have replaceable cartridges and limited output capabilities. If you find vendors talking about "replacement needles," then you generally don't have a unit of high enough quality for any serious project. There are turntables on the market that, in addition to having RCA output connectors, have dedicated USB connectors. An ancillary benefit of the USB-out turntables is that they have the necessary pre-amp and equalization devices built right in, so all that is necessary is to plug them into the wall and then into the computer. Often, they are sold as an "out-of-the-box" solution with the cartridge mounted to the head shell and already balanced, the cartridge selected to particularly mate with that turntable. Again, the Audio-Technica mentioned early is a good choice, particularly with the lower-mass cartridge that they have been using.

As with any piece of audio equipment, how much you choose to spend can be a major determinant of the product you can purchase. An entry-level product can often be purchased for under $100 (depending on where you purchase it from). For this, you will get a basic turntable with an integrated cartridge/head shell and a belt-driven platter. Belt drive units are less costly to manufacture, and the belt has the added benefit of absorbing some of the motor noise and vibration. A downside is that belts stretch over time and may need to be replaced; also, they frequently take one or two revolutions to get up to full speed: a feature that may be a hindrance if the recording has some "close cuing" to do. Also, these entry-level units may not have very effective **resonance** isolation characteristics, meaning that they can be susceptible to ambient room noise or vibration that can be picked up and passed along to your recording. This can be reduced by having the turntable on a separate desk from where the speakers are located or placed on **acoustic feet**.

Moving up in the "food chain" so to speak takes us to the next level of turntable. Typically these are direct-drive units, which means the turntable platter itself is a part of the motor; they are designed so the motor resonance is below that of the audio level or the ability of the stylus to pick it up and they get up to speed in as little as one-third of a revolution. They also typically have a more stable platform that is more resistant to room noise and vibration. Often they are supplied with a cartridge that is uniquely designed for that turntable, but if necessary, the user can "swap it out" for another one, a particularly useful feature if one is going to be transcribing a large number of older and 78 rpm discs. These older discs pre-date the "**micro-groove**" format and had deeper grooves. A stylus designed for a micro-groove disc could "bottom out" or not accurately track the wider groove of an older album, resulting in poor audio performance. Again, consult a reputable dealer for guidance. If you need to change the stylus/cartridge, you may need to realign it to the head shell. To the uninitiated this can be a frustrating task; oddly enough, an "older" person who has done this process may be your best source.

Another benefit of a higher-end unit is, aside from improved sound quality, the build quality is better. You will find a higher level of electronics and motor as well as tone arm and mechanisms. Again, a downside to this is that you may have to set up the unit, a daunting task even for those experienced in turntable setup. Fortunately, many new units designed for USB output are designed for the DJ or club environment and often come already setup, with only a few user adjustments needed. Higher-end units also will have a more stable speed management system. This system controls wow and flutter. "**Wow**" is exactly what it sounds like; it is a slow change in the rotation speed of the turntable that can alter the lowest notes on a record. "**Flutter**" is the complete opposite; it is short speed variations that can impact the upper reaches of your records. Wow will be more noticeable on recordings with significant bass content such as organ music or recordings with double-bass solos. Flutter will be more noticeable on recordings with sustained piano notes. Better units will have a **quartz-locked** or some other speed management device, while lower-end units will depend on the 60Hz cycle of the standard outlet to maintain correct speed. Often, this is shown by the use of a **strobe light** on the edge of the turntable illuminating dots or ridges on the edge of the platter. When the dots seem to stand still, then the turntable is theoretically turning at the correct speed, subject to the limitations of the governing device. This method is dependent on the quality of the line service; in most cases, electric utilities go to great lengths to make certain the frequency is stable as electric motors depend on this. Be aware that the "line load" on the circuit or even in the building if the circuit is dedicated can impact the accuracy of the line frequency. Turntables that have strobe speed lights will usually have *four* rows of dots; one row for 33⅓ and another for 45 rpm at **60Hz** (the standard in the United States) and another two rows for the same speeds but at 50Hz (the standard in Canada.)

There are just a few (I promise!) other things that you need to be aware of with turntables. One is ***tracking force***. This is the downward force that a stylus presses down on a record album with. Too much and the album will be damaged and high-frequencies often rolled off; too little and the sound will be distorted and the needle may jump out of the groove on some dynamic passages. The amount of tracking force that is correct is determined by the cartridge/stylus arrangement. These numbers will typically be supplied by the manufacturer of the cartridge. Another adjustment, one that works in conjunction with the tracking force, is ***anti-skating***. When playing a record, a needle will have a natural tendency to want to move toward the center of the album. Anti-skating is a force applied to the tone arm to counteract this. It "pulls" the arm outward in an amount equal to cancel out the inward force; this keeps the stylus in the center of the groove and with equal wear on both sides of the stylus and groove. It typically is a function of the tracking force. The correct value will be specified by the turntable manufacturer in conjunction with the cartridge specifications. Tracking force is typically adjusted by installing and balancing the cartridge and stylus in the head shell. Then, the **counterweight** on the back of the tone arm is rotated until the tone arm is "balanced"; that is, it does not move up or down when left alone. Then, holding the counterweight with one hand, the force ring is turned to the value of "0" and then the ring and counterweight turned to the specified value. It

Figure 5.10 A tonearm counterweight and anti-skate adjustment gauge. (c2.staticflickr. com)

can be confirmed via the use of a **stylus force gauge** that can be obtained at better audio-video stores.

On figure 5.10, the counterweight and the anti-skate is circled.

The last thing we are going to cover is ***cueing***. Cueing is simply the method whereby the tone arm is lowered to the record surface. This needs to be done gently as too abrupt or fast of a contact will damage the record and possibly the stylus. Most turntables have a lever at the back or base of the tone arm that can be used to lift and lower the tone arm. Frequently these actions are "dampened" so that the tone arm raises and lowers slowly. Depending on the turntable, you may need to both lower the tone arm at the beginning and raise it again at the end of the recording. This would be the scenario found in a ***manual* turntable**. If you need to manually place the tone arm at the start of the record (or selection) but the turntable lifts the tone arm at the end of the piece (and may place it back in the tone arm holder) then the turntable is said to be ***semi-automatic***. This is the great majority of better-quality turntables on the market; it does require some additional mechanics but is more convenient and can help prevent album/stylus damage by a tone arm left circling at the end of a recording. If the turntable lifts the tone arm and places it down at the beginning of the album and then lifts it off at the end, this is said to be an ***automatic* turntable**. Again, with the added convenience comes increased complexity. Some units are designed to assume a 33⅓ rpm recording is 12 in. and a 45 rpm recording is 7 in. (yes, these numbers are not "RDA compliant," but it is the way they are described in the audio world); deviate from those standard sizes and the function will not work properly. Some have an independent record-size selector. Most high-quality turntables will be of the semiautomatic variety; depending on your budget, this may be the most prudent way to go.

As to cost, whereas a basic belt-driven USB turntable with a basic quality cartridge/style will go for around $100, a good direct-drive semiautomatic unit with a high-quality cartridge and computer-locked speed mechanism can go for around $400. (Of course, if you want to get some *really* exotic platters/bases/cartridges, prices can easily exceed $5,000 but those are the domain of the high-end audiophiles who, surprisingly, are often not married. Go figure!) If you are comfortable with the technology and equipment, then feel free to order a unit from a *reputable* online vendor. If going this route, check the reviews for a unit that fits your needs and price range. Go to that vendor's site and see if it sells direct or if it lists authorized local retailers/online vendor sites. It is important to stay with those sites as you are assured of factory warranty support if necessary and you know that you are getting the genuine article, not a cheap look-alike knock-off, something all too common in this Internet age. If working with an online vendor, check to see if it has a "chat" feature or a number where you can call and talk with someone; there are some very good dedicated

Internet-based companies that offer good service and prices; two that the author has worked with are *LP Gear* at www.lpgear.com and *Turntable Needles* at www.turntableneedles.com.

If you are not comfortable with ordering online or sight unseen, then go to a local retailer or specialty store. There are many reputable "**big-box**" stores that carry good units, or you may need to go to a specialty audio shop; if you go the latter route, you will typically get a better product with better aftersales support, but at a price.

At this point, you may not be certain what path you want to go down, so here is a suggestion. If you are just "getting your feet wet" and not certain if funding or institutional support will be there, then go with a "basic" unit from a mass-market retailer. This will help you get a feel for the technology and the process without a major investment in time or money. If you decide to move forward with the project, then you can invest in a better, higher-quality unit. In the short term it may cost more, but in the long run, it can prevent you from spending money on a project that isn't "green lit" by the funding agency, so you can cut your losses.

This is one of those points where the distance between the paragraphs doesn't do justice to the process. You've devoted time to getting hardware and everything set up, either via a direct-connect turntable or via a turntable/receiver combination and have it plugged into your computer (and your computer "recognizes" it at the USB port). If your computer "sees" it, try playing a record through the speakers. You may need to go into the control panel and select it (the control panel may think it is a microphone) but if you hear music, you are good to go.

WORKING WITH RECORDS (LPS)

Sadly, one cannot just pull an album out of the jacket, throw it on the platter, and start recording. Records are not as durable as more modern mediums, so they will require extra care.

First, wash your hands with a good soap and water and dry them with a cotton towel. They don't need to be "sanitized," but a good cleaning is preferred. In fact, using waterless hand sanitizer is *not* recommended as they often contain alcohol, and alcohol is the enemy of vinyl records. Then if there is any plastic **shrink-wrap** on the **jacket**, remove it. The plastic holds dust and will impart that dust to the disc when you take it out as well as put pressure on the jacket and potentially warp the album. If you have put the jacket inside plastic holders, remove them also. While good for protecting the jacket and album when circulating, they are not good for long-term storage, and honestly, take up a lot of space.

The best way to get an album out of the jacket is to gently tilt the open end of the jacket downward so gravity pulls the album onto your free hand. If the album is in a **sleeve**, then remove the entire sleeve and album (as a hint, when putting it back, place the album in the sleeve and then place the sleeve with the open end *up* when placing it back in the jacket; this will protect it from dust in the future and make it easier to take out the next time you wish to play it). Put the jacket down and tilt the sleeve so that the album moves down onto your hand. Place your thumb on the outer rim of the album and support it with your middle finger on the inner label. Take your other hand and place it on the label opposite to your first hand gently holding the album between your two hands, rotating it if necessary so that the correct side is "up." Now gently lower it onto the **spindle**. *Do not* press down on the album. If the spindle isn't directly below the hole, try to "look down" through the hole and line it up. Try not to put the record label on the spindle and "hunt" for the hole by moving the album around; this can warp or break the album and the subsequent "**hunt lines**" can reduce the collector and archival value of the album.

Figure 5.11 One way to hold a record album. (www.dreamstime.com)

Figure 5.12 Another way to hold a record album. (www.dreamstime.com)

With the album on the turntable, you should clean it. Resist the temptation to blow on the record; this can cause condensation on the album that can cause dust to adhere. That "click" or "pop" you hear when playing an album is often caused by the stylus "running into" a speck of dust, so we want to get rid of as many of them as possible. Some people recommend a "wet" cleaning, particularly if the desire is to get one good play out of the album for digitization purposes. Under this method, a soft cloth has distilled water on it and the record is cleaned in a concentric motion. Remember, go *with* the grooves in a circular motion around the album, *not* in a radial line running from the center to the edge as one would with a CD! Doing so will scratch the album. Allow the record to dry before playing it.

Most audiophiles still feel the best way to clean a record album is with a purpose-designed brush. Obviously, this brush cannot be obtained at your local supermarket. Go to your local big-box audio store, boutique audio/

video seller if you have one, or perhaps a local electronic store and purchase a good cleaner. If you are serious about a good product, look on eBay or online for a product called **Discwasher®**. At one time, this product was considered *de rigueur* for record cleaning. Using Bing or another search engine, it is still possible to purchase the product new, but it is not as "elegant" as it was in the 70s and 80s, though still the best album-cleaning product around. This product,

Figure 5.13 The Discwasher record cleaning system.

along with the accompanying D4® fluid, wet-cleans, stabilizes, and dries the record surface. It is one of those products that should be in the arsenal of anybody transcribing record albums. Ironically, a very good (and comparable) product can be purchased at Urban Outfitter stores. Urban Outfitter has a strong commitment to vinyl, and while it may not have the original Discwasher product, it has a comparable product that does an excellent job.

At this point we are going to pause in the recording process to look at another frequently used input device, the cassette deck.

CASSETTE TAPES AND TAPE DECKS

One of the most numerous items in a library's nonprint collection, at least from an historical perspective, is audio cassettes. Developed by the Philips Corporation, the original product was designed to be a "low-fi" tool, designed for simple voice recording and office transcription. It soon became popular outside the office environment and soon found its way into homes, cars, portable use, and just about every part of the recorded world. With increasing popularity, the desire to improve the quality of the product soon consumed the research efforts of many different companies and individuals.

It's odd that the cassette should become so aligned with quality audio reproduction. The tape width is quite narrow, the tape itself is very thin, and the tape housings do not lend themselves to high-quality sound reproduction. It was those attributes, however, that led to the success of the cassette. It was highly portable and it could be designed to hold 90 minutes of music in a reasonably durable format. From a manufacturing point of view, it would eventually be possible to design and build equipment that could duplicate the contents onto a tape from a master in as little as 20 seconds (high speed indeed!). With development of the Dolby Noise Reduction System®, the greatest drawback of the format, tape hiss, could be greatly reduced; improved tape formulations, such as **Chromium Dioxide (CrO_2)** and **Ferro Chrome (FrCr)**, also helped contribute to extended dynamic and frequency range and lower noise.

The portability and availability of good-quality portable recording devices led to their widespread use for recording live events, from sermons at church to birthday parties and baby's first words. They were often found, sometimes, in a slightly more advanced format at school and college musical performances along with speeches and presentations given by visiting dignitaries and notables. Their low cost, good quality, widespread adoption, and ease of duplication (even at the local level) made them a favorite of many educational and community groups. So popular, in fact, that many were made, hopefully labeled, and stored away, never to be cataloged unless they were considered of historical note.

Today we find these odd cassettes all over our libraries, many containing little more than a notation that says *1998 Spring Concert* with little else on them. If you are lucky, there may be some information as to the selections performed, who composed them, and who performed them, but more often than not, those facts are not written down on the item or in a log anywhere. The portability that the cassette brought to oral historians is significant. Many scholarly, and even more amateur and self-appointed, historians took their recorders and captured the thoughts of an age; of survivors of the Great Depression, the World Wars, of life in Appalachia, rural farms without any electricity or running water, people who had never seen a book or a movie but had generations of family history stored in their head. Now that information could be captured in their own voice, their own words, in an inexpensive, good quality, easy-to-use format.

Fortunately, some of these tapes were labeled, cataloged, organized, and perhaps even had transcripts made. Many more, unfortunately, were tossed into a box, perhaps on a shelf, maybe in a drawer or cabinet, sometimes labeled, oftentimes not, to await "someone" to make use of them. At the time, those who made them assumed they would always remember what was on them, or that it would be "obvious" from the material on them that any listener would know what it was. For those items that were labeled and documented, we now have the means to make more user-friendly and sharable copies; we can transcribe them into an electronic form that can be burned to a CD and duplicated with ease, giving the user the benefit of "chapter access" so if multiple interviews or dates are on a single disc, they can directly go to the one they want. More importantly, we can take these digital files, create metadata for them, and make them accessible through finding tools on websites; with increased proliferation of broadband and portable access, users can now access these bits of history from home, their office, the library, their car, even their phone. All that needs to be done is for us to digitize them.

Setting up a cassette deck isn't quite as complex as a turntable, but there are still some technical and functional issues that users need to be aware of. When setting up a turntable, if you went with the receiver/tuner option, then connecting a cassette deck won't be that difficult. If you have a good-quality existing cassette deck, all you will need to do is connect the *out* RCA connectors on the cassette deck to the *in* RCA connectors on the receiver. From there, you can use the existing connection from the line out on the receiver to the computer; to record from the cassette deck instead of the turntable, all you will need to do is select the source that you connected it to on the back of the receiver and you are ready to go. As with turntables, it is also possible to purchase cassette decks that have a USB out connector; they are available at many office supply and online AV supply companies.

Note that there are only four connections that we need to be concerned with, two out and two in, but to get the sound to another device, we are going to use only the *output* or *play* connectors.

A good-quality cassette deck is important. First and foremost, it should be one with a good motor able to play stereo sources at a constant speed. If exotic tape formulations such as CrO_2 and FeCr are used, then there should be an option for using them. Absolutely critical will be a cassette deck that has the Dolby system on it. If the deck bears the Dolby symbol (a pair of capital "D"s facing each other), then it has the necessary circuitry.

How do you know if a tape was recorded using the circuitry? If, when playing the tape, you hear a high level of tape hiss and the high-frequency sounds seem unnatural or unbalanced to the rest of the sounds, then turn the Dolby option on; if it sounds normal, then it was recorded with Dolby. If you have it turned on and the sound is muffled and has no high-end, try playing it with Dolby turned off; if it sounds normal, then it wasn't recorded with the Dolby circuitry. Most "portable" cassette recorders did not have the Dolby feature, it being reserved for home or more high-end units. Of course, this is all predicated on the fact the tape is still in good condition.

Cassette tapes, for all their durability, do not handle environmental extremes very well. High heat can cause the tape case to warp and not feed the tape properly. High heat can also cause delamination of the base from

Figure 5.14 The back of a cassette deck.

the magnetic layer, resulting in adhesive preventing the tape from playing. If a tape does not play when putting it into the deck, try gently tapping the tape shell a few times on the edges; also try putting the tape into the deck and fast-forwarding and rewinding it a few times to loosen the tape pack. If the tape seems good but the shell and hubs are bad, it is possible to transfer the tape pack to a new shell, but practice on some noncritical ones before doing this with sensitive or historical items. If a tape makes a high-pitched screeching sound when playing, you may be out of luck; the tape has been stretched or damaged beyond repair. Moving the tape pack to another shell *may* help as may winding the tape back and forth a few times, but generally, the tape is beyond repair. Some have insisted that if the tape is heated in an oven (not a microwave) for a few minutes, it may result in a tape that gives you one or two good plays, but this author has never tried it and some say this is more urban legend than audiophile fact. Good-quality tapes generally hold up better than the old "three for a dollar" packs that were so popular in the 60s and 70s, as are shorter (60- and some 90-minute tapes) as opposed to the 120- and 180-minute tapes that some used; on those, the tape is just too thin to be durable.

Like a turntable, a cassette deck requires some basic maintenance. If the drive motors are in good shape, a simple cleaning may be all that is needed. Using isopropyl alcohol and a cotton swab, clean the tape heads and pinch roller. The **pinch roller** is the small rubber "wheel" in the lower right-hand part of the tape well. You may need to have the deck on and press "play" to expose the heads and wheel to adequately clean them. Be careful to not allow cotton strands to wind around the pulley or the capstan. Use the same alcohol to clean the heads.

If the deck has not been used in some time, or after every 30 or 40 hours of use, a ***demagnetizer*** should be used on the heads. These devices are available

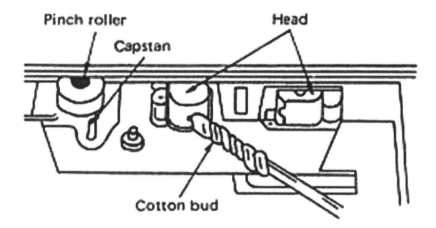

Figure 5.15 Cleaning the tape-path parts of a cassette deck.

at most electronic supply stores. When using them, make certain that *all* audio and video cassettes are at least 10 feet away as stray magnetic energy from the demagnetizer could cause distortion in the source material. When using the demagnetizer, follow the directions that come with it; each model works a bit differently. Under *no circumstances* should you use a commercial cassette cleaner unit. These devices which look like cassette tapes are designed to be put into the deck and "played" for 20 to 40 seconds. While convenient, they often contain abrasive tape that can damage the heads and the pinch roller; if you have one, throw it away *now!*; it isn't worth the risk. Tape heads should be cleaned approximately every 20 to 30 hours of tape play time; more if you are playing poor-quality tapes. There are two schools of thought as to when to clean the heads. Some say directly before making a critical recording, others say immediately after playing a low-grade cassette; generally, it doesn't matter so long as the alcohol on the heads is allowed to air dry before playing a tape.

OTHER AUDIO SOURCES

Connecting and recording other sources, such as reel-to-reel, 8-track, or any other analog source isn't significantly different from a record album or a cassette. For these items, all you really need to do is connect their line-level output to the receiver and use that to route the signal to your computer. If you don't have a receiver/tuner, you could try connecting the outputs of the source (provided they are RCA connectors) to your RCA-to-USB adapter and capture the sound that way into your computer. You may need to make some level adjustments in the recording software, but typically, if they are line-level outputs, you should be just fine.

A word of caution. *Do not* use an RCA to mini adapter and connect the output of the source device to the microphone input of your computer; the level is typically too high and will result in distorted and poor-quality sound. It *may* be possible to attenuate the input, but generally, you will not get acceptable sound quality this way. If the output of the unit (particularly older portable reel-to-reel recorders) looks round with six small holes in it in a ¼ circle, it

Figure 5.16 A typical DIN connector.

may be a **DIN connector**. Any good electronics store can supply you with a DIN to RCA connector which you can then use to connect to your receiver or USB adapter.

RECORDING SOUNDS

Now that you have decided what source you are going to use and have it connected to the computer, let's go through a short demonstration. For the purposes of this demonstration, we are going to use a turntable as our source. To begin with, let's look at some of the buttons used in the recording process.

Figure 5.17 The basic Audacity toolbar.

This is the basic toolbar used in Audacity. Let's look at some of its integral parts.

Figure 5.18 The Audacity navigational buttons.

These are basic navigational buttons used during recording and playback. They function similarly to those on a tape deck. (Depending on the version you are using, you may not have all these buttons or they may be in a different order.) The functions are, moving from left to right:

Figure 5.19 The PAUSE button.

PAUSE a recording. Use this if you are not done with a recording but need to "take a break" or turn an album or tape over.

Figure 5.20 The PLAY/REPEAT button.

REPEAT a portion of a recording. Use this if you need to hear a cut multiple times. It is not used during the recording process.

Figure 5.21 The STOP button.

Use this to *stop* a recording. Use this *only* when you have completed a recording. Once you press this, you *cannot* continue with the recording. You *can* make a new recording and paste it onto the original, but it is not efficient.

Figure 5.22 The JUMP to the begining of the recording button.

Figure 5.23 The JUMP to the end of the recording button.

Figure 5.24 The RECORD button.

Press RECORD to start the recording process. Audacity will start recording as soon as you press this button. For ease of use, you may want to start the recording process *before* you put the stylus on the album. Don't worry about any noise, you can delete that portion of the recording when you are editing it.

The next group of options allows you to determine the input and output formats of the sound. Typically, the only option you will need to use here is the one to the monitor the input sound process. You will need to do this *every time* you launch Audacity:

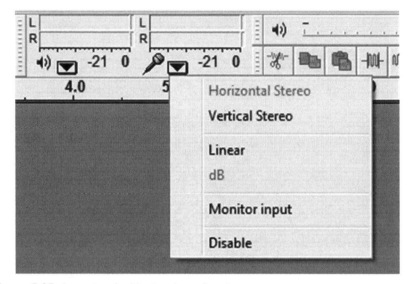

Figure 5.25 Accessing the Monitor Input function.

This menu is accessed by clicking on the drop-down arrow by the microphone. Click on the Monitor Input option to listen to the recording while you are making it. Be certain to not turn the volume up too loud; otherwise you may get feedback or distortion through your source device.

These bars are used to monitor sound levels. You cannot adjust these bars; they are for monitoring purposes only. When recording, use the slider bar to the right of the microphone on the top line to adjust the recording level so that it doesn't exceed the range of the bars.

During the recording process, you can adjust input levels and balance by using the input level controls as shown in figure 5.26.

The first slider (the one with the − and + on the right and left of it) allows you increase/decrease the input level. Use this control gingerly. If you set it too high, you will cause the sound to "clip" and be distorted. Move it too low and it will not be loud enough.

The "L-R" slider control sets the relative balance between the two channels. You may need to adjust this based on your experience, but for now, leave it at the default position. Initially, you may wish to use headphones to get a sense of "left and right" balance before relying on the speakers.

This toolbar provides access to file storage, manipulation, and modification of the recorded signal. It operates similar to other Widows-based toolbars.

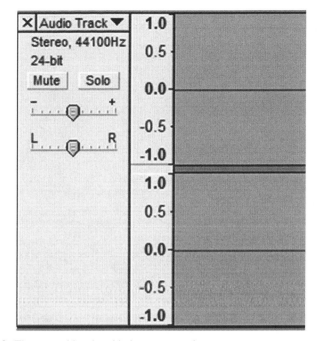

Figure 5.26 The record level and balance controls.

Figure 5.27 The file manipulation and modification toolbar.

THE RECORDING PROCESS

Click on the RECORD button to start the recording. Pause as necessary. *Do not* click on the STOP button until you are completed with the recording. As a general rule, do not create a file that is over 62 minutes in length. While CDs *can* hold more, the potential for a failed burn increases as you get closer to the 70-minute mark. Also, longer files can take longer to process; if necessary, break longer items (e.g., 90-minute cassettes) into two separate scans.

Immediately after you click on the STOP button, save your recording! Audacity treats every recording as a *project*. To save your *project*, go to File, Save Project, and save your recording. To simplify the saving/editing process, you may want to create a folder on your computer with a name like "Audio-Raw" and save the file there. When you are done editing it, you can move the file(s) to their permanent location. Do not make this working file an external hard or network drive; there may be performance issues that could crash the process. Once you have saved the recording, you can begin the editing process.

EDITING YOUR RECORDING

This will allow you to edit your recording to get rid of some noise or to make any other enhancements.

Figure 5.28 The editing toolbar.

The most common buttons you will use are Edit and Effect buttons. The Edit button tells the software *what* you want to change, and the Effect button tells the software *how* you want to change it.

1. The first thing you will want to do is *normalize* the recording. This helps "synchronize" both track and remove any phase shift errors in your computer's sound card. If you are creating a low-quality recording, such as for a portable MP3 player or podcast, then you can also reduce the dynamic range of the recording.

    - If you are making archival recordings, you will save the "raw" recording with no edits to preserve its integrity, but you will still need to do this step; it does not alter the *sound* but rather adjusts for any deficiencies in the computer's sound card.
    - Select the entire recording by clicking Edit, Select, All, or CTRL + A. This will highlight the entire recording.
    - Click on Effect and select Normalize. To retain the dynamic range of the recording for editing, deselect the *normalize maximum amplitude to-1db* and check the *Remove any DC offset (center on 0.0 vertically)* and click on the OK box. We will return to this box later on to get the recording to the maximum output level for the target source. This will help "even out" the sound levels of your recordings (not within the recording themselves, but across multiple recordings).

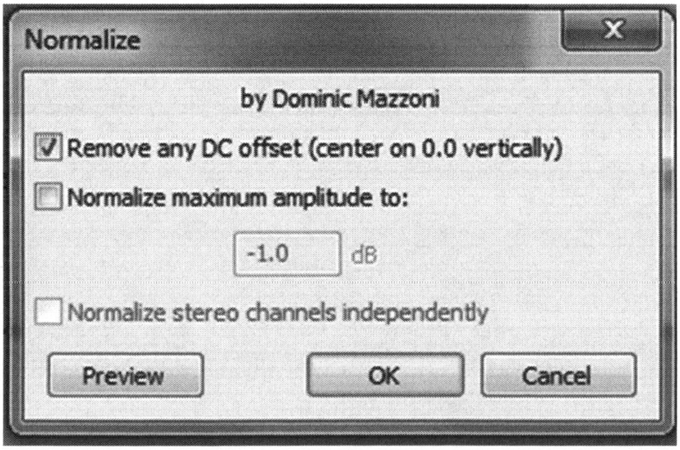

Normalize ✕

by Dominic Mazzoni

☑ Remove any DC offset (center on 0.0 vertically)

☐ Normalize maximum amplitude to:

[-1.0] dB

☐ Normalize stereo channels independently

[Preview]   [OK]   [Cancel]

Figure 5.29 The Normalize effect box.

- This process typically will not take long, depending on the speed of your computer. If you are going to create an archival *and* a working/release copy, *export* the file as a single track as covered in the end of this section and save the project, then re-load the Audacity file so it can be edited for your working/release copy.

2. The next step is to remove any surface noise that you may have. This is useful if your original recording has a lot of surface noise, such as a record album or tape, or if you have a lot of background ambient noise.

   - To make this process fully effective, Audacity recommends that when making a recording of a record album, you place the tone arm on the album, *then* start the platter rotating. The author experience has used this method but doesn't support this recommendation.
   - Select a short portion of the recording where there is no recorded information. Typically, this will be at the very beginning of the recording.

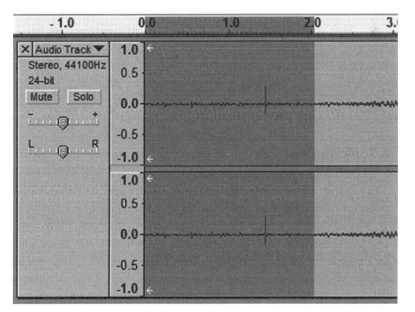

Figure 5.30 Selecting the baseline noise area.

- The darker areas are where the software has been told "this is an area of no noise, this is what a 'quiet' portion of the recording sounds like." You will notice that in this area there are some noise artifacts; This is a good thing as it will help Audacity remove the noise in the rest of the recording.
- Click on Effect and Noise Removal. Click on the *Get noise profile* box.
- After the software has obtained the noise profile, go back to the recording and select the *entire recording*.
- Go back to Effect and Noise Removal. *Do not* click on the *Get noise profile* box again or else you will *erase* your entire recording.

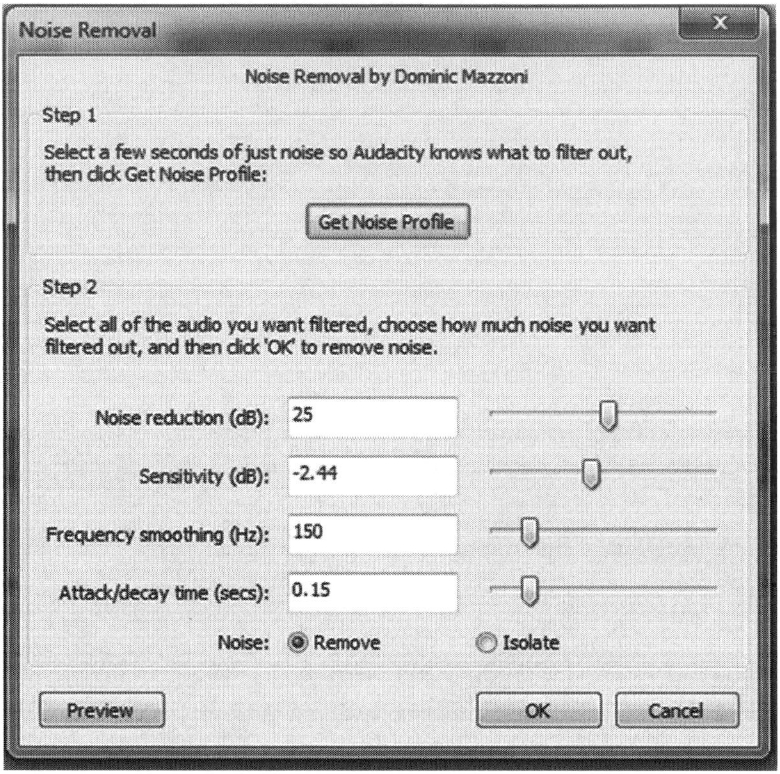

Figure 5.31 The Noise Removal profile box.

- Depending on the noise level of your source, you may wish to move the *Noise reduction* and *Sensitivity* sliders more toward the right side, but try not to go more than half-way there until you have a better feel of how aggressive the noise removal will be; as a general rule, when in doubt, opt for a less aggressive solution; if it is not enough, you can go back and redo the process with a more aggressive option, or you can click on the Preview button to see how aggressive your results will be. When you have selected the values, click on the OK button and the process will begin. Over time, you will learn what is a good choice based on the noise level of the source recording. The software will then remove the noise from your recording. This process may take up to 10 minutes, depending on the length of the recording, the amount of noise that has to be removed, and the speed of your computer. Remember, after running the process, you can see the results. If they are not satisfactory, you can go to the Edit tab and *Undo Noise removal* and try again.

3. To remove scratches from recordings, select the entire recording, then Effect, Click Removal and accept the defaults there. Be careful not to be too aggressive with this option. If there are a few clicks that are problematic, then only highlight those clicks and select a more aggressive option individually. Yes, it takes

longer, but it helps preserve the integrity of the recording. Note, you typically won't need to do this with recordings from tape sources unless the tape itself is made from a record album. Click on the **OK** button to run the program.

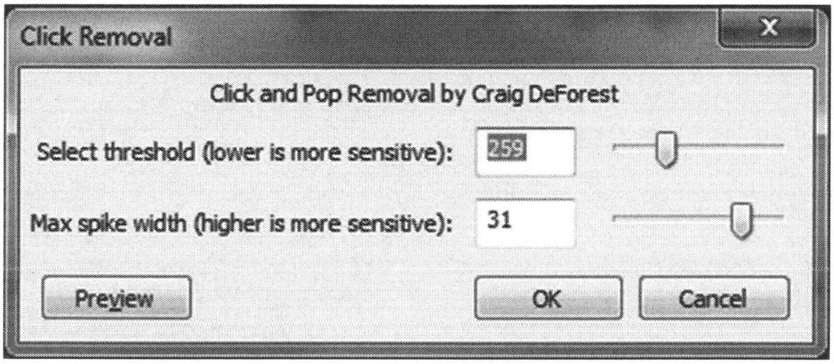

Figure 5.32 The Click Removal box.

4. If the recording has low bass content as many older recordings do, you can re-equalize to add more bass by selecting the entire recording, then Bass and Treble from the effects menu. If the recording is going to be played over "full range" speakers, as might be found in a good home sound system, try not to go above 6 on the slider with the *Gain* no higher than 7. When in doubt, use the Preview button to see what your results will be. Remember, you will need to be using good-quality speakers or headphones to get an "accurate" sound. Again, the defaults typically work quite well.

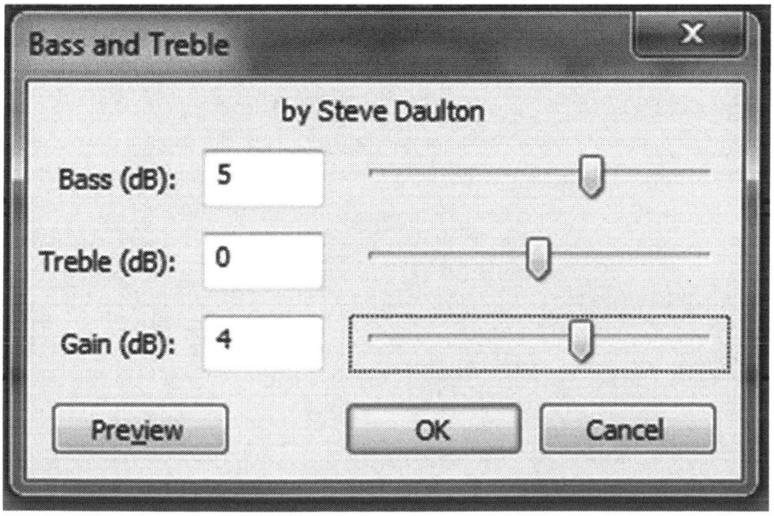

Figure 5.33 The Bass and Treble adjustment box.

5. If you want to delete any sections, such as long breaks caused by pausing when you turned the record or tape over, extensive sections at the beginning or end of the recording, or particular part of the recording, this is the best time to do it. Simply highlight the section you want to delete and press the Delete key on the keyboard.

6. At this point, if you are done with editing and don't want to include chapter tracks, then you can save and export the file as shown later. To insert chapter tracks and burn a CD or store on some other device, proceed as below.

7. Go to the beginning of the recording and insert a track stop by clicking at the begging of the selection and then going to Tracks and then Add Label at Selection. This will place a small notation box at the bottom of the screen.

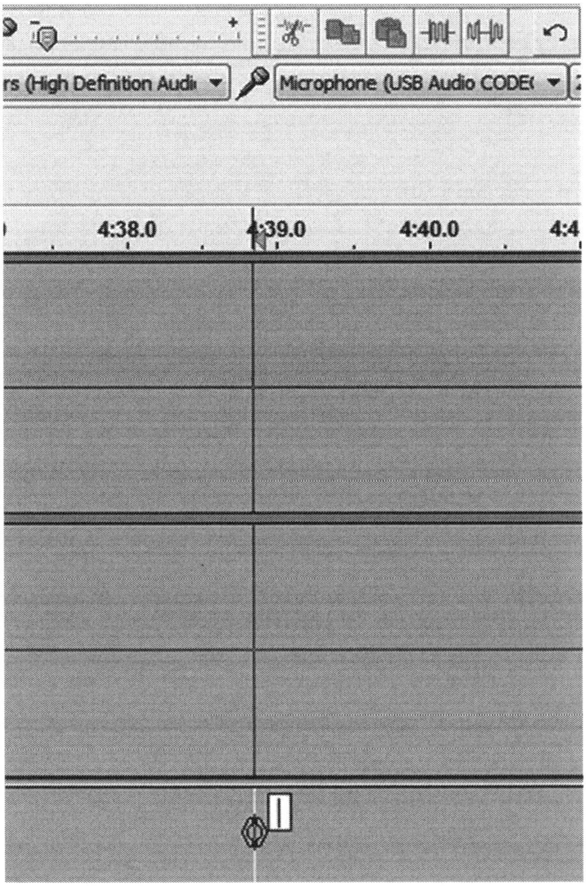

Figure 5.34 Inserting a track break.

- As this is the first track, place your cursor in the box and type *Track 1*.
- Using the scroll bar, scroll until you come to the next place you want to insert a track label. If you need to, you can minimize the recording display by clicking on the magnifying lens on the toolbar.

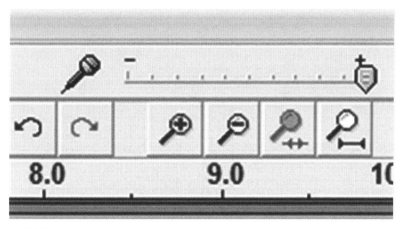

Figure 5.35 The magnifying lens buttons.

- Generally, you can recognize logical "breaking points" by the absence of signal between two pieces of music or sound. The cursor on the picture indicates one such place.

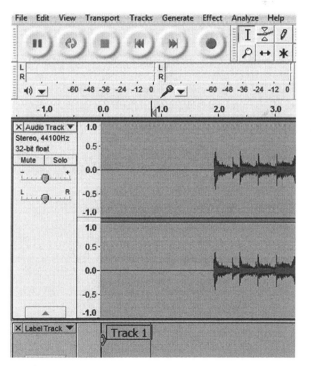

Figure 5.36 Identifying tracks.

- To be certain this is where you want the break, you can move the cursor back to just before the break, click on the Play button, and when you get to the point you want to insert the chapter break, press the Pause button. If you don't get it right the first time, don't worry; you can repeat the process until you are satisfied with the results.

- NOTE: After you insert the track number, you will need to click on the Stop button before you can continue editing.
- If you need to remove a track, place the cursor at the end of the track label and press the Backspace key removing the notation. After all characters have been removed, press the Enter key to remove the notation.
- When you are done entering track numbers (the typical maximum you can enter is 23), remember to save your project.

7. At this point, we want to maximize the level of the recording, so we burn it at the maximum volume possible. After adding the chapter stops, type *CTRL + A* then click on Effect > Normalize.

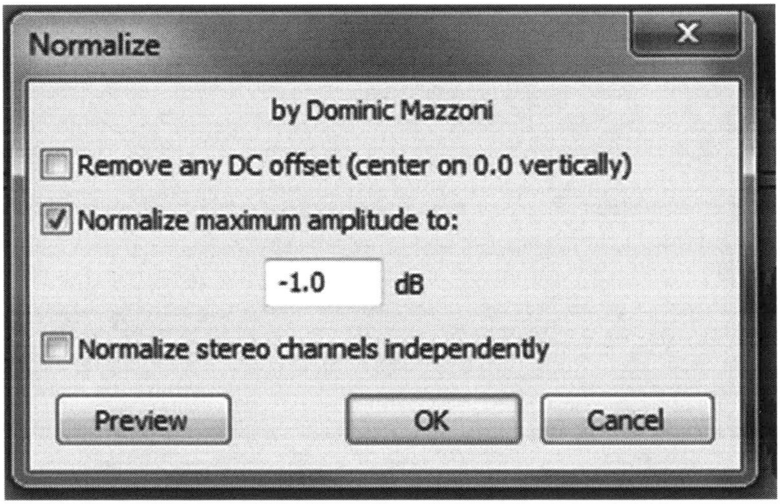

Figure 5.37 The Normalize box.

- Uncheck the *Remove any DC offset (center on 0.0 vertically)* and check the *Normalize the maximum amplitude to:* and leave the value of *–1.0* in the box. Do not check the *Normalize stereo channels independently.* Click on the OK button.

EXPORTING YOUR WORK

At this point, you are reading to export your work. If you are exporting for MP3 or a podcast and there is only a *single track*, then click on File, Export as MP3. A dialogue box will open prompting you for the location and name of the file.

If you are exporting for a CD or with multiple tracks, then click on File, Export multiple. This will open a dialogue box. From the drop-down menu in the *Export format* area, select *WAV (Microsoft) signed 16 bit PCM*. Make certain the other radio buttons are selected as indicated. Specify a path to save the recording and click on the *Export* box.

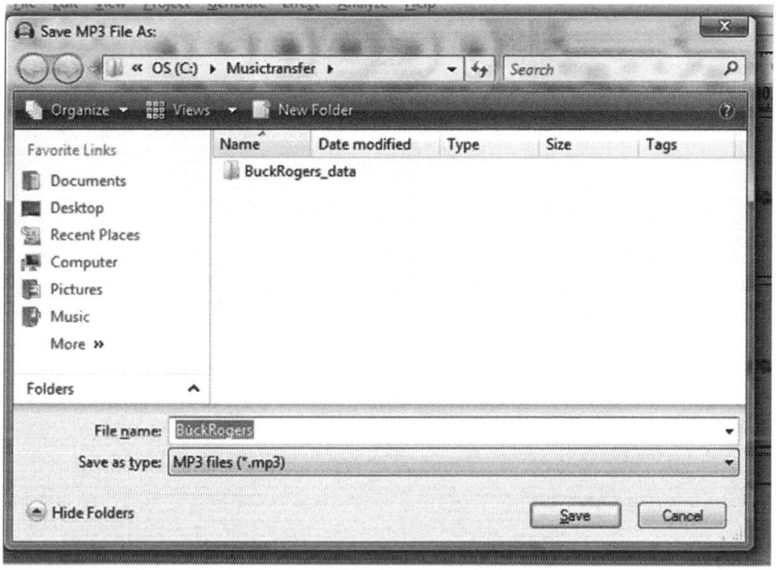

Figure 5.38 File export dialogue box.

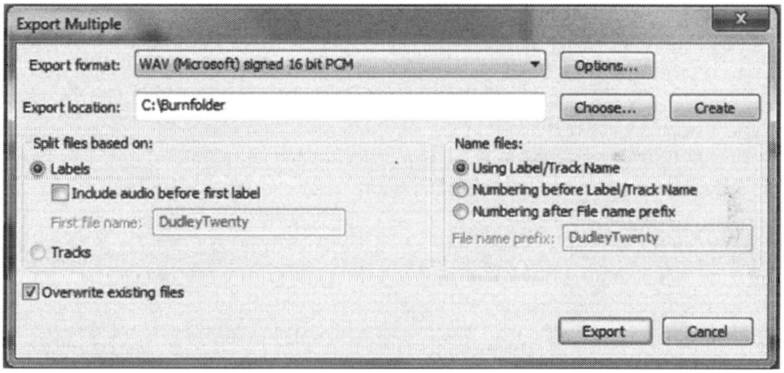

Figure 5.39 Exporting multiple files.

This will bring up the Edit metadata box as shown in figure 5.40.

Make certain the number in the *Track title* area and the *Track Number* area agree. If they do not, you will need to go back and verify that you have numbered the tracks correctly. This box will appear after *each* track is saved, so verify for each track. If it matches, click on the OK button.

This will export the tracks you have created as WAV files to the destination you specified. If you do not intend to create a CD or other physical manifestation, then you can move those files to your online long-term storage environment, such as an external hard drive or network drive. If you are going to create a CD, continue with the following instructions.

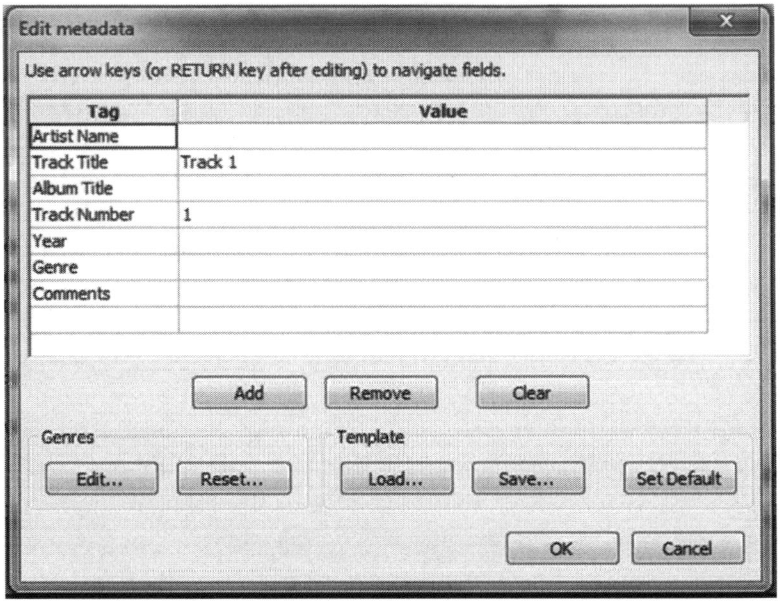

Figure 5.40 The Edit metadata box.

CREATING A CD

Note: These instructions presume that you have access to a CD burner and are using a CD-R disc. Do not use CD-RW discs as they will not yield as durable results and may not play in some standalone CD players. Depending on the software you are using, your process may be different. For the purposes of this exercise, we will be using *Windows Media Player 10*.

1. Minimize the Audacity software and launch Windows Media Player. After launching Media Player, click on the Burn tab.
2. Open the folder where you have the tracks stored. Highlight all the tracks and drag them into the area of Media Player where it says Drag items here.

Figure 5.41 Draging files to Windows Media Player.

3. After the items are in the burn list, you can close the folder where the files are. You will now see the files are in the burn list, but they may not be in numerical order:

   • You can sort the tracks by either dragging them in the correct order, or using the Burn options tab and sort them by Title.

4. After the tracks are in the Burn list and there are no errors (no duplicate track numbers, etc.) click on the *Start burn* button to burn your CD. The software will burn your CD as well as finalize the disc.

5. Make any labels that you wish. Move the files from your working directory to the final location, either on an external device or on a network drive.

Play	Burn	Sync

Start burn   Clear list

CD Drive (D:)
Audio CD

28:09 free of 80 mins

Burn list

Disc 1 (51:48)

Track 12	2:47
Track 13	2:13
Track 14	2:18
Track 15	2:56
Track 16	2:12
Track 17	2:17
Track 18	3:39
Track 19	2:54
Track 20	1:54
Track 1	2:08
Track 2	2:30
Track 3	2:11

Figure 5.42 Audio files in the Burn menu.

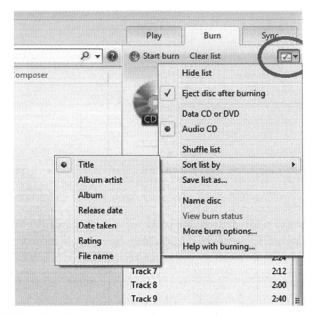

Figure 5.43 Ordering files by title in the Burn menu.

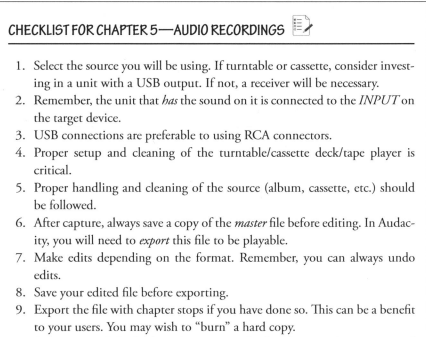

CHECKLIST FOR CHAPTER 5—AUDIO RECORDINGS

1. Select the source you will be using. If turntable or cassette, consider investing in a unit with a USB output. If not, a receiver will be necessary.
2. Remember, the unit that *has* the sound on it is connected to the *INPUT* on the target device.
3. USB connections are preferable to using RCA connectors.
4. Proper setup and cleaning of the turntable/cassette deck/tape player is critical.
5. Proper handling and cleaning of the source (album, cassette, etc.) should be followed.
6. After capture, always save a copy of the *master* file before editing. In Audacity, you will need to *export* this file to be playable.
7. Make edits depending on the format. Remember, you can always undo edits.
8. Save your edited file before exporting.
9. Export the file with chapter stops if you have done so. This can be a benefit to your users. You may wish to "burn" a hard copy.
10. Save a copy of the final product on your backup location (server, external drive, etc.)

Chapter 6

Video Recordings

The basic premise for digitizing video recordings is similar to that for sound recordings, just a lot more complex. With sound recordings, one only has the sound; with video recordings one has sound *and* picture. To capture the full bandwidth of both with good quality requires as much computing power as can possibly be dedicated to the task. In addition, since there is now the dimension of video, one will have to take into account the fragility of the physical medium. While larger, VHS cassettes have much more that can go wrong with them since the information is not just recorded on the *surface* as in audio cassettes but is actually layered within the magnetic tape; some information is on the surface, some is below. Coupled with the fact that there may be multiple tracks for sound in addition to the picture and the fact that the tape moves across a spinning head complicates matters.

VIDEO RECORDING FORMATS

VHS recorders work by passing the ½ in. tape at a given speed over an angled spinning head. The process of threading the tape around the head is the sound you hear and causes the delay from the time you press the PLAY button and the tape actually begins to play. If you want to fast-forward or rewind quickly, pressing the STOP button and then the REWIND button means that the player has to unthread the tape before it can fast wind it. The accuracy with which the tape is aligned to the spinning head has a major impact on picture quality. Even a slight misalignment can cause distortion in the playback. Older VCRs had a device called a *tracking* adjustment that allowed the user to make fine adjustments to the head/tape alignment. Most modern VCRs perform this process automatically.

With the appropriate tape/speed configuration, it is possible to get eight hours (or more) of information on a tape, but as with all things, there is no free lunch. The increased playing time comes at the expense of quality and accuracy. The three most common speeds are **SP** for **Standard Play** yielding two hours of record/playback time on standard tape, **LP** or **Long Play** which would give four hours of record/playback time, and **SLP** or **Super Long**

Play, which would yield six hours of playing time. There is another speed, often called **ELP** or **Extended Long Play**, that would yield up to eight hours of playing time, but at significant degradation of signal. This format is typically only found in specialized applications, such as security systems where repeated playings are not the norm and tapes are recorded more for archival storage and limited reference rather than regular usage.

Commercial videotapes would typically use the two-hour mode, giving the best quality and was a good choice since few movies would run over two hours. If the movie did so, the production company would either use a slower speed and sacrifice quality or use two tapes and charge a higher price. Most homemade video recordings made with a camcorder would often be at the two hours speed as people were seeking to create the best possible image, often of a baby's first steps or some special event; many home off-the-air tapings were done at the four-hour mode: a speed that yielded acceptable quality for most off-air tapings while giving four hours of playing time.

While ½ in. VHS (and to a much less extent, ½ in. Beta) was used in most home and school environments due to cost, there were some "early adopters" and broadcast environments that would use ¾ in. U-matic tape. U-matic was a broadcast standard that held up to one hour per tape at normal speed and quality. Since the tape was larger and ran at a faster speed, the quality was typically better than that found with ½ in., or "**broadcast quality**," that is, quality suitable for television and cable broadcasting. Some school and college media departments invested heavily in the ¾ in. format, particularly if there was a broadcast program. Ultimately, technology, cost, and convenience would outstrip the format, and VHS became the standard. This is not to say that ¾ in. died off; on the contrary, there is a very large archival base of ¾ in. recordings out there, recordings of very high quality and many times professionally captured. These recordings frequently are of visiting dignitaries, speakers, and special events; the events often being of such note that the best in technology and manpower would be dedicated to capturing the events. Many institutions have extensive collections of these recordings, but many do not have a functioning player any more. The good news is that they are still able to be purchased in the used market; the bad news is the price is often north of $1,200 for a good unit. If you need to borrow one, check schools in your local area; they may have one or two sitting in a storage room unused; ask if you can borrow it, although it may need to be "refurbished" before use.

Predating the ¾ in. U-Matic even further are reel-to-reel 1 in. tape units. These are true "broadcast" units used in well-funded and/or high-quality environments. As with the ¾ in. units, the picture and production quality are typically very high due to the inherent strength of the format and its support structure. As with ¾ in. units, players can still be found, but at very steep prices.

Finally, the last format we are going to look at are laserdiscs. These were developed by the Pioneer Corporation as the next step in high-quality home video. Their strength was superior picture quality to VHS units and, depending on the recording technique used, could offer up to two hours on a single disc. They used a digital format for sound (up to five **discrete** channels) and an analog format for video. As the name implies, the pickup device was a laser beam. With proper mastering, they could deliver a sound and picture experience that far exceeded that possible with videotapes. What made them popular with educational institutions, however, was that they were not a liner format. This means that to go from one part of a show to another or one could often "jump" to that point without having to fast-wind past the other parts. With educational titles, some dedicated players came with a barcode scanner that could be used to scan the barcodes in an instructor's manual to jump directly to a particular scene. Some discs were used to contain thousands of still images from art galleries and other similar sources.

Laserdiscs had their drawbacks though. First and foremost, they were quite expensive. Their design precluded high-speed duplicating as could be done with videotapes. It wasn't until the development of compact discs (CDs) was a way found that they could be stamped as record albums quickly rather than having to be "burned" in real time. Second, the players could be quite expensive since they didn't find widespread acceptance in the home market; this limited the numbers that would be produced, increasing the cost-per-unit. Third, if not properly manufactured, they would suffer from *video rot*, a phenomenon that would cause the disc surface to delaminate from the substrate and render the disc unplayable. Because of their nature, it is rare that an institute will have a locally recorded disc. The only time an institution may need to transcribe one is when the original content is no longer available and the copyright holder has given permission to make a transcribed copy.

For a short time, there was another competing disc format marketed by RCA called **SelectaVision**. It used a needle in a groove to reproduce audio and video signals. The tolerance that it worked with was very tight; the disc was kept inside a plastic case that was fitted to the front of the player. The player then pulled the disc out of the case into the player for playback. After playing, the player would put the disc back into the case. The tediousness of this process worked against the widespread adoption of the format, although a few discs can be found. Connecting the player would be identical to any other video format.

If these paragraphs have taught us anything, it's that there is no "free lunch." If one wants high playing time, then there will be a sacrifice in quality and vice versa. Convenience will often be offset by higher cost or a non-durable format. Each format has its strengths, and each has its drawbacks. The unfortunate part is that a library or archive may have multiple formats and multiple qualities. The good news is that once one understands the basic precepts of capturing these formats, the same basic techniques can be used for all the other formats. Typically, one will use the same RCA/S-Video to USB connector for all formats. Once you get the technique down for one, the same skills can be applied to another. If one has multiple formats to work with, it would be advisable to do all of one format before moving on to the next format, if for no other reason to obtain proficiency with that format.

AUDIO-VIDEO (AV) CAPTURE SOFTWARE

Unlike Audacity, there is no really good comparable free product for capturing video recordings. The user will need to look at the different products available on the market to determine which one works best for him or user. When looking for software, consider the following features:

1. Does the software permit the manual insertion of chapter stops?

   • This can be important when transcribing long recordings. Remember how annoying it was to have to fast-forward to "that spot" on the tape that you wanted to show. With this feature, one can put a chapter stop in the exact location(s) one wants and go directly to those using the standard search and jump functions in most playback units. Be clear on this feature though; some software says "insert chapter stops," which means that the software can automatically insert a chapter stop for every 10 minutes of playing time regardless of location. While this feature can be turned on or off; the user is not able to specify exactly *where* each stop is. More preferable is software that allows the user to insert chapter stops where he or she wishes them to be. Typically, the maximum number of stops that can be inserted on a single disc are 99.

2. Are multiple record times supported?

   • Some software is limited to one hour of record time, some to two hours, and some are limited only by how much storage space you have. As a general rule, anything with a limit under two hours is not going to be adequate for most projects; anything with over two hours may not be useful but isn't going to do any damage. Remember, video recordings will consume a significantly larger volume of space than a sound recording will. As an example, a 72-minute concert video will require approximately 3GB of data, and a 90-minute movie will require 3 ½ to 4GB of data. This is the *raw file* that you will have to capture, *not* the final file. The size of the file is dependent on how much information is in the original, such as scene changes and action. The more action and scene changes there are, the greater the size of the file. The size of the final file is determined by a variety of factors, including playing time, compression used, and type of recording; live-action concert footage will require more space than standard movies because of the format used by DVDs to store data.

3. Is the software able to split longer recordings into smaller segments?

- This feature can be important if you have long recordings that you want to break down into smaller chunks. Some software packages cannot do this very well, some can do it very easily, and some don't do it at all.

4. Does the software allow for varied recording times?

- Remember, a DVD has a finite recording space and is inherently a "lossy" format. DVDs (and Blu-ray discs) are able to accomplish their prodigious recording times because they use a variety of techniques to save space. There are some recordings on the market that are notorious for having dropouts during some scenes because the format is presented with too much changing information too quickly. The more you try to "**compress** down" a recording, the more the quality will suffer. Some software packages will present you with the time of your recording and then show you the implications of compressing the signal. As a *general* rule, you will get the best quality with no more than two hours per DVD. Some editing tools will give you an indication of how long the final file will be. If it exceeds the limits of the disc, it may offer to compress the file to fit the available space, but remember, you will be sacrificing quality.

5. What editing facilities does the disc offer?

- Some institutions will want to create "professional-looking" products, complete with title frames, scene selection menus, and so forth. Remember, while they can be useful, they will increase the cost of the software and the time required to master a disc. Furthermore, some older players may not support these features because they are not commercially made. When editing a video, does the software show the actual edits or are they stored in a file and only applied during the internal burn process?
- A good (and free) resource is Microsoft's *Movie Maker*. It allows you to do some special effects, titles, credits, and others. While free and relatively easy to use, it is strictly an ***authoring*** tool. It cannot be used to actually burn the resulting file to a disc; this may be a consideration if you are wanting to create physical discs for your users, although it can output the file to a hard drive/server for importing into your video management software.

6. What is the output format of the software?

- Does the software permit multiple output formats such as .MPEG, or is it strictly a proprietary format? If it exports a standard format, is another piece of software necessary to actually burn the disc? This is not a major issue as there is a large body of very versatile software available at minimal cost that will allow the conversion of a file from one format to another (from .MPEG to a format for an iPhone, for example, and vice versa). This last feature can be quite useful if one has video from a smartphone. With the proper software, it can be loaded into your video capture software and edited there for burning/archiving.

7. How complicated is the software?

- No matter how functional the software, if it is difficult to use the feature *you want*, then you will become frustrated with it. It's not about what features the software has and how easy they are to use; what is more relevant is whether the software has the features *you* want and they are easy for *you* to use.

There are many products on the market that support the process. Most come with a connector that has up to four female connectors on one end (two for audio, one for video, and an S-video connector) and a male USB connector to connect to your computer, although the connectors are readily available at any good audio/video parts store.

Some products to consider:

http://www.vhs2dvdwizard.com/?tid=B19

VHS2DVDWizard is a good product. It has two separate components. The first is the capture software that moves the image from your source to the computer and offers basic editing functions; the second is a more powerful editing package that allows customized chapter stops, merging of videos, splitting of source material, titles, and the like. Support is quite good; it is a package this author has used for many years.

http://www.roxio.com/enu/products/creator/device/overview.html

Roxio is a company known for its audio and video tools. Again, the product comes with all the hardware you need, although you may need to download some specific drivers. The author has not used this particular package, and it has had mixed reviews, so make certain you have a trial period, if possible, or be willing to work with it for a while.

https://www.diamondmm.com/vc500-diamond-one-touch-video-capture-edit-stream.html

The Diamond VC500 product has received many good reviews and it is very reasonably priced. Again, the author has not used this product, but there appears to be a very good support structure for it and the system requirements it lays out can be useful.

Personally, this author has gone down the path of converting over a hundred sources and did exhaustive research on the various products available to do the conversion. One package this author recommends based on personal experience is *VHS2DVDConverter* sold online by Quick Click Software. The package is reasonably priced, can be as simple or complex to use as the user wishes, and is able to handle multiple input forms and can do the DVD mastering and burning directly without another software package. As a side benefit, it includes an RCA-to-USB converter and has responsive and professional software report. Note that this paragraph is only the experiences *this* author has had with the product. There are other products out there that may be just as good; check with trusted sources before investing in a software product.

To move recordings to a DVD, there is a multistep process that you will go through. These steps are:

1. **CAPTURE**: This is where you take the image from the *source* and capture it on your computer using the video capture software. Most software indicates between 600MB and 3GB for every hour of video captured.
2. **EDITING**: This is where you will edit the captured file and make any changes you need to, such as eliminating excessive introductory or lead-out blanks, or, in the case of laserdiscs, "blue screen" where you had to turn the disc over. Typically, this will take the bulk of your time.
3. **MASTERING**: This where the software "masters" the source material into the DVD format. It is important to remember that the DVD is only a carrier; how the information is stored on the disc is distinct from the carrier. The mastering process is critical to the storage of the information due to the algorithm that DVDs use to store images. As a *general* rule, live concert or action footage will require more disc space than a simple interview with a person or group. Also, if you do any compression, the process will take longer. During the mastering process, you should not run any other processes on your computer.
4. **BURNING**: If burning the image to a disc, this is the actual process of burning the finalized information to a disc. Depending on the source material it can take half as long to 1¼ times longer than the source to burn.

> ***Reminder:*** when capturing and editing video, do not use that computer for any other task, including automatic updates or reminders.

A very important consideration to remember when capturing video is that your computer should not be doing *any* other tasks. Video capture is an extremely processor- and memory-intensive process, demanding the full resources of hardware, memory, disk drives, and other resources. It would even be wise to disconnect the computer from the Internet and turn off any automatic updating software. Also, turn off any "hibernation" functions as your computer may not recognize something is actually happening and "go to sleep" in the middle of a capture. In Windows, there are multiple power settings. It's a good idea to create a setting for "video capture" that prevents any sleeping or hibernating and devotes all system resources to the task at hand. True, it may slightly increase power consumption, but the tradeoff is an uninterrupted and accurate capture.

When viewing the raw files, you may notice some "artifacts" around the edges of the screen or certain images on the screen, such as "halos" around singular bright light sources. The artifacts around the image are often "leftovers" from the **NTSC** scanning process used in older television and video recordings as well as actually capturing some "overhead" data that broadcasters used for maintaining color accuracy across a network or to signal automatic equipment to an upcoming commercial or content break. Again, for accuracy's sake, it would be wise to retain this for future researchers. The halo effect can either be an artifact leftover from the limitations of early generation cameras or simply the inability of the computer display to render an accurate image. Very often, when the content is finally mastered and viewed in a "standard" viewing environment, they will go away.

There are multiple ways one can go about capturing the original image. Unlike audio sources, there are not "USB compatible" video players out there, at least not for the formats we want to grab. Given this, there are two routes that we can take.

The first is similar to what we did with the audio recordings. Frequently, the software that you purchase to do the capturing and editing will come with an RCA-to-USB adapter. If you go this route, then you will need three male-to-male RCA connector cables and the adapter. The three cables will plug into the audio out (red and white/black) and the other into the video out (typically a yellow connector) on the back of the source player. The other end will plug into their corresponding counterparts on the RCA-to-USB adapter (note that some adapters support S-video; if this is an option, then go this route as the picture quality will typically be better). Then plug the other end of the adapter into the USB jack on your computer. Windows should "recognize" the input, and the software will typically be able to sort it out. When making the connection to the USB port, *do not* go through a **USB hub**. Connect directly to a USB port on the computer; hubs may not offer the necessary throughput to produce uninterrupted recordings.

Another option would be to plug the video source into the receiver/tuner and then take the output of the receiver/tuner to the computer using the patch cables. This can have the benefit of simplifying going from source to source if you are using multiple sources, but depending on the age and quality of the equipment, there may be some signal degradation. If the equipment is newer, bypass any "signal enhancement" options for both audio and video. While it may seem desirable to have the best quality signal possible going to the computer, it is important to remember that the signal that you are presenting to the computer has been artificially enhanced: not an option if you are desiring to create an "honest" copy of the source.

On the back of this receiver, the video input/output connectors are circled. Note that video connections typically are yellow.

The audio inputs are circled here. Remember, to match the correct audio/video sources for each so that when you select that source, the audio and video from the source will match.

As with any project, test your process on a few "non-critical" items before moving on to more important sources. One feature of some mastering products is that you can specify the level of compression you will need to apply to the source prior to burning. If you notice that you have to do a significant

Figure 6.1 The video connections on the back of a receiver.

Figure 6.2 The audio connections on the back of a receiver.

amount of compression, consider splitting the capture into smaller segments; by trying to get too much onto a single disc, you will be sacrificing image quality.

After capture, *always* save the raw captured file to a drive that is regularly backed up. As a matter of good archival principle, you should always keep one file for future research that has not been edited and is as "raw" as possible. It is perfectly acceptable to make multiple secondary formats for physical distribution as well as for distribution over the web (such copies may be stored at a lower bit-rate to facilitate streaming), but ultimately there should be a "master copy" that future researchers can go back to for critical research purposes.

If you have made a physical disc, such as a DVD, take the DVD and actually play it in a noncomputer-based DVD or Blu-ray player. This is important as it confirms that the disc can be played in a noncomputer environment. This is because DVDs contain various pieces of "overhead" information used by players. It also helps to test any chapter stops and/or title/menus you may have placed at the beginning. During some of these playbacks the captured image may look "better" than what you saw on the computer screen. Frequently, this is caused by the DVD "**upconverting**" the image to a higher resolution level. Obviously, the picture cannot have higher resolution than what was originally captured, but the player can create the illusion of better by spreading the picture out over a smaller number of "pixels" or dots on the screen, giving the impression that there is less "dark space" between each of them and that they are closer together, thereby making the picture look "better" than what was originally captured. Furthermore, depending on the type of TV you are using, the TV may have some type of image-enhancement or noise-removal process. Again, while not "accurate" they can result in a more aesthetically pleasing picture.

CHECKLIST FOR CHAPTER 6—VIDEO RECORDINGS

1. Locate a player for the source you wish to convert. If a VHS video recorder/player, it may be prudent to have it cleaned prior to use. As with cassette players, *do not* use tape cleaning units you "play" to clean the player.
2. Make certain you have plenty of disc space. Allocate 3GB of space for every hour of recording.
3. Select the software you will be using. Make certain it is easy to use and can do the editing you wish.
4. Assemble any necessary connectors. Most editing/conversion packages come with the necessary RCA-to-USB converter.
5. Capture no more than two hours of video at a time.
6. Allow plenty of time for editing.
7. When editing is done, master the final version. This can take a long time, but fortunately, you don't need to be sitting at the computer when this is being done.
8. Burn your final copy and/or export to an external secure device/server.

Chapter 7

Finishing Up

By now you have captured a recording or two, perhaps some videos, did some editing, maybe burned a few physical artifacts, but there are a few things we need to remember on a going-forward basis.

STORAGE

Original Sound Recordings

Before putting any sound recordings away, it is important that you store them correctly. For record albums, this means taking any plastic shrink wrap or other plastic jackets and sleeves from off of the jacket. While seemingly helping to protect the album, they actually contribute to its degradation. Shrink wrap is exactly what the name says: "shrink wrap." It is shrunk to the album cover, thereby putting pressure on the contents, which serves to warp and put stress on the jacket. Furthermore, dust clings to it, so when you remove the album, the dust along the edges of the shrink wrap is transferred to the album.

Another consideration is the record sleeve. The best option is simple paper sleeves; if the sleeves are damaged, then they can be replaced with archival quality sleeves. If the sleeve has a plastic lining, it is better to replace it. Sleeves that have an **onionskin** lining are generally acceptable. Again, the plastic can hold dust and, if it becomes too warm, can leach into the album. When storing record albums, it is best to put the album into the sleeve, then place the sleeve into the jacket with the open end up, at a 90° angle to the opening of the jacket. This will help prevent dust from getting on the disc surface during storage and when it is removed.

When storing albums, they should be stored vertically, snuggly packed together; not too tight, not too loose. They should not be leaning at an angle and should be supported on both sides by full-panel supports rather than wire brackets one might use for books. Standard room temperature between 65° and 74° Fahrenheit (18° to 23° Celsius) with moderate humidity is optimal; too dry and static charges can draw dust to the disc surface. Generally, a too humid environment is not a danger to the album itself but to the paper jacket; if the jacket should warp, it can put stress on the album, thereby warping it. The nominal number of record albums that you should have is no more than 6 ½ to the linear inch.

Cassettes should be stored in a hard-shell case. Some advocate that the case should be stored open-end down to prevent compression of a particular reel, some advocate a vertical storage position with the full tape-pack up, and others advocate a flat storage. This author's experience has not found any method that is "better" than the other, aside from placing them in a case or cabinet with dividers for each cassette, preferably of nonmetal construction and away from any magnetic sources and bright lights. Humidity should not exceed 60 percent with any cabinets bearing the weight of each shelf, not the cassette cases.

Reel-to-reel tapes should be stored in acid-free boxes vertically just as one would store record albums. They too should be stored in a location away from metal and no more than 60 percent humidity.

One of the challenges of any magnetic medium such as cassettes or reel-to-reel tapes is that they should be "refreshed" at least once per year. This can be something as simple as winding them from start to finish and back again, slowing the winding as it gets toward the end of the tape pack. If a cassette shell becomes damaged or the "slip sheets" inside fail, or the tape guides, then a replacement shell can be obtained and the tape pack moved to the new shell. The process is not difficult; just be certain not to use any metal tools in the process. Also, if a tape should become broken, try to avoid splicing it as the splicing tape can contain adhesives that will "bleed" over time. A better option would be to move the two parts to new shells with short leader sections attached.

Original Video Recordings

Like cassettes, ½ in. and ¾ in. tapes should be stored in a hard-shell case for protection. They should be kept away from metal or any magnetic sources and should be "refreshed" once per year and stored in an environment similar to cassettes and record albums. Open-reel tapes should be stored in a cardboard box in a similar environment that one would store reel-to-reel tapes. If a tape inside a cartridge, such as a VHS or Beta tape, take it to a professional to repair; improper repair can damage both the tape and the player.

Laserdiscs should be stored similar to record albums. Remove any plastic shrink wrap and store insert the sleeve at a 90° angle to the opening of the jacket with the sleeve opening facing up. One area that laserdiscs differ from record albums is that they may have a sleeve of rice paper. For laserdiscs, this is better than a paper sleeve as the edges of a paper sleeve can cause concentric scratches that can render the disc unplayable. Like record albums, however, they should be stored vertically with the open toward the back of the shelf to help seal against dust and with any end supports full-size, not wire brackets. Since they are thicker than record albums, you should typically have five discs to the linear inch. Contrary to urban legend, because laserdiscs are an *optical* format, magnets and metal shelving will not damage the content on the discs.

Other Formats

For items like player piano rolls, music box discs, 8-tracks, digital compact cassettes, the same storage rules apply as for their cousins as listed earlier. Anything that uses a magnetic tape is susceptible to metal and magnetic fields. The best way to store most items is in a secure acid-free box in a temperature- and humidity-controlled area. Like their print counterparts, however, many (but not) all older formats are more resilient and durable than their modern cousins owing to the more stable materials used in many (but not) all formats.

OUTPUT FILE STORAGE

Up to this point we have devoted most of our time to playing and capturing of our sources along with manipulation and physical output of our work. The assumption has been that most people engaging in these types of projects will have some background in archives management and procedures, but for the sake of all users, some of those principles will be covered here.

You will have noticed that during every capture process, as soon as the item was captured, it was stored so that there would be a "master" file of our work. For some products such as Audacity or video capture, it would be wise to export them to an "industry standard" format. This is somewhat a misleading term since what was considered to be "industry standard" as little as five years ago is unreadable today. This is compounded by the fact that some products, such as Audacity, store the file in a proprietary manner. As was covered in the chapter on sound digitization (chapter 5), it is best to save the following:

1. A full copy of the original recording made by the capture software.
2. An exported version of that file in a more widely available format, such as. **WAV files**. WAV files are a good choice as they are loss-less and, being a Microsoft product, have the *potential* for long-term viability. Avoid any lossy formats such as **ACC**.
3. Save a copy of the fully and final edited file both in a hard format and in an electronic format, preferably in multiple locations.
4. When completed, store a copy of all the files generated in steps 1, 2, and 3 to *both* a server environment and at least *two* external formats such as external hard drives *and* DVD/CDs. At least one copy of all files should be stored off-site in a secure locations. Any files stored on a server should be backed up in a **"Son-Father-Grandfather"** arrangement with proper storage off-site at a secure location.

As you can see, these steps are very time-consuming and, by definition, costly. It is possible that one could reduce the number of off-site files stored, but since the files are not dynamic they won't need to be rotated on a regular basis, except for those stored on a server that may also contain other information.

One caveat about being stored on a server, even though it is backed up each night, is if the backup software utilizes any data compression (most do.) Depending on the methodology, the process could introduce artifacts or loss. This is why it is good to have an external physical copy of the file. The old stand-by "**WinZip**" is actually a good choice as it is a loss-less format, although it is not the best for audio formats as the compression rate isn't as high as some dedicated media-specific formats.

One consideration that many have made is to store data "in the cloud." While seemingly cost- and time-effective, there are various legal and financial issues with this. While this publication does not purport to offer legal advice, some of these considerations are:

1. Who owns the data in the cloud and who is responsible for it? What if the vendor's cloud environment "crashes?" What financial compensation will be offered?
2. What about security? Who has access to the data? Does the vendor have the right to "crawl" the data for research and information purposes? How is it encoded against data breaches?
3. If the library chooses to end the relationship with the vendor, how will the vendor return the data? Many libraries have found that in their contracts that they may own the data, but the vendor owns the encryption and formatting rights, enabling it to charge an "export fee" for the library to get its own data back.
4. What about data compression? Some vendors, to save space (and money), will compress the data. Is the compression lossy or **loss-less** and is it proprietary to the vendor?
5. Depending on the project, will **mirror sites** be available? What is the throughput capabilities of the vendor taking into account the Internet and/or your local network?

Again, this publication does not purport to offer legal advice, but there are other considerations that you will need to make regarding your project. Some of these are:

1. Access. Depending on any copyright issues, will users need to be "on site" to access the original and/or edited copies, or can they be accessed remotely? Will off-site users only have access to a "degraded" version of the product but have to come to your facility to access the master and edited versions, or will the edited versions be available remotely but the master version available on-site only?

2. How many simultaneous users will be allowed? Depending on server/network capacity you may allow only a specified number of simultaneous users. Legal restrictions may allow only a single simultaneous user; if so, you will need metering software to control this.

3. Are there geographic limitations? Are the resources allowed outside your city/state/country? Again, if there are limitations, you will need software to control this.

4. Will fees be charged? If so, a collection mechanism will need to be created.

5. Is your library part of a digital consortium? Can your files be loaded/displayed/searched there? If so, are those guidelines and standards consistent with those in your own library, or do you have to conform to the hosted sites' standards?

INFORMATION ACCESS

In the "olden days" this book would have talked about how to create **MARC** records for the information. While useful, MARC has been supplanted by many tools, such as Dublin Core, Mods, Fedora, Access. Each has its strengths and limitations. The following points are enumerated, not to suggest a specific product or methodology, but to help structure the thinking of those who need to create and store the information as well as how it can be harvested.

1. What resources does the library have at hand? Is there funding for dedicated software or will the library be compelled to use an "off-the-shelf" product? Perhaps state or local standards mandate the software that is to be used to receive funding-agency approval for participation in a shared-project venture.

2. If the library is using a **discovery tool**, what ability does that tool have to "crawl" the data encoding system? Most of the systems from the larger library vendors are able to crawl a variety of systems, particularly those that are library-based. You may need to work with the vendor to develop a model so that the date is stored in a manner consistent with your other data sources. This step *cannot be stressed enough!* In the past, we depended on our library catalogs, or **OPAC**s as the chief finding aid in the library; now, discovery tools have taken over many of those tasks, particularly since they can present many diverse and different databases in a single, consistent results page while offering limiting options and suggested searching strategies.

3. Will you be using a standard taxonomy, or will you be creating one of your own? While it may sound advantageous to create one of your own, this brings with it another set of problems. You will need to create and maintain a database of those terms and make certain that all involved in the project adhere to those terms. If new terms are needed, who will develop the terms? Is there a "governance" structure in place to make certain that the created terms are consistent in form and structure with previously created terms?

- Many catalogers and project managers have bemoaned the inconsistencies and limitations of some vocabularies such as *Library of Congress Subject Headings* (LCSH) and its counterpart the *Library of Congress Name Authority File* (**LCNAF**), and while some of these arguments are valid, the ubiquity of the vocabulary helps bring consistency among users across libraries as they search for terms. Of particular importance is the participation of the Library of Congress in the *Virtual Internet Authority File* (**VIAF**), which has the potential to simplify searching across multinational databases.

- Consider the benefits. By using a vocabulary and structure that a significant portion of your other datasets (most notably your catalog) you make your discovery tool that much more powerful in its ability to collocate items from different information sources and enhance its ability to suggest related terms and improve the relevance ranking of resultant searches. This is particularly significant if the discovery tool is able to access authority records linked to the data records as the authority records can help the discovery tool suggest broader and/or narrower terms or alternative terms completely. If, under the idea of linked data, library systems are able to harness the power of the VIAF, then it is theoretically possible that users coming into your system from outside the United States will be able to user their native search terms (at least for names at this point) and be redirected to the correct form in the United State, with users in this country having the reverse potential to explore databases in other countries.

- Not every name that you use in your project will be in the LCNAF, to be sure. This is particularly true if you are working on local history projects with the names of people and places not in the LCNAF or LCSH. If this is the case, then by constructing names and subjects that are *consistent* with the forms in the two Library of Congress databases, it will aid the discovery tool in indexing and presenting the data in a consistent manner as well as aid your users by providing consistent search input structures so that searches are more successful. While not suggesting that every library become a *Name Authority Cooperative* (**NACO**) approved library, it would be a beneficial move to look at some of the documents and examples in the NACO protocols when constructing names and headings; this will assist both the discovery tool and the users in having a consistent data form to work from.

4. Will the data be stored "natively" or in another finding tool? This point may seem moot after Number 3, but there are scenarios where a library does not have a discovery tool. In these situations, the library will need to decide if it is going to create all the data in a MARC structure in the catalog, or it is going to create the data in another "finding aid." If the latter, then a means needs to be created to get users from the catalog to the finding aid. Many libraries will create a single MARC record in the catalog that "points" to the finding aid, some will create a separate website for the project, and some will adopt both methods. The benefit of this method is that it allows the use of a purpose-developed tool for encoding,

manipulating, and presenting the information. The downside is that it forces users to look in two different places for information, increasing the chances that some researchers will miss desired resources because they are in "the other system" with no cross-walk provided between them. It also means that staff will need to be hired/trained in maintaining the alternative site.

5.   Who will do the data creation, and what provisions are made for quality control? Oftentimes the task will fall either to a cataloger or to a similar metadata specialist. This person is skilled in the use of controlled vocabularies and the ideas of access points and description. Of particular use are the resources developed by the *Online Audio-Visual Catalogers organization* (**OLAC**) as they specialize in the metadata creation for nonprint materials. They can be found at www.olacinc.org. The downside is that a cataloger is often constrained, either unconsciously or by training, to thinking only in MARC and Library of Congress terms and is not able to "make the leap" to other structures. Another organization you may wish to consider membership in is the *Association of Moving Image Archivists* (AMIA). As stated on its website, http://www.amianet.org/ it is "established to advance the field of moving image archiving by fostering cooperation among individuals and organizations concerned with the acquisition, description, preservation, exhibition and use of moving image materials."

*   On the other hand, by utilizing a subject specialist for the metadata creation, the person creating the data is not limited by the ideas of strict vocabularies, which can also be the problem; they are too close to the subject matter, particularly in areas of local history, to be "objective" in creating data that is consistent with other forms of data in the library. A "compromise" solution, obviously, is a collaboration between the two. The subject specialist or historian/archivist may suggest terms, while the cataloger subsequently is able to "translate" these terms and ideas into forms consistent with other library resources. Obviously, this method is more labor intensive, but it will aid in creating data that is consistent across the library's various platforms.

THE FUTURE

Many times we have touched on the future, but it bears repeating here. There need to be provisions for data maintenance, for those errors that will inevitably creep into the project, for the "redoing" of some samples, and, in some projects, the ability to add to the corpus of work already created. Depending on the initial plan, the project could be "closed ended." This is recommended since you will know when you have completed the project and obtained closure; nothing is more frustrating and morale-wrecking than a project that just seems to languish with no "endgame" in sight. Even if there is another "project" similar to the one just completed, it is important to have a definite end in sight, if for no other reason than to call attention to the project by having the ability to "celebrate" that it is completed. This can be a powerful tool for obtaining funding for future projects.

Also, it will be necessary to lay out a plan for long-term data maintenance. Admittedly, this topic has been covered before, but it bears repeating. What are the prospects for long-term funding? It is often easy (admittedly, a relative term) to obtain funding to *do* a project, but funding agencies rarely are interested in funding the *maintenance* of a project. Often, funding agencies will want to see what provisions have been put in place for the long-term viability of the project. Will the parent organization assume funding responsibility for data maintenance and migration, or will the project become "static" and languish? If the latter, then all that work will be "frozen" in time with no ability to migrate it to latter platforms or search structures, ultimately running the risk of becoming obsolete.

More important than the technology, what about the people involved in the project? If a critical person leaves, retires, or is unable to continue with the project, what provisions have been made for their intellectual contributions? Even with good documentation, a significant portion of any project exists in the minds and creativity of the people involved. Ideally, a period of transition is desirable if someone has to leave the project, but sometimes fate intervenes in the form of an illness or accident and the person is not available to aid in the transition. In technical areas this is not as critical, but even in areas as basic as data cleanup and formatting it can be critical as each person's "ear" and "vision" may be slightly different; this subtle changes can be quite small at first, but can migrate to larger differences over time. When comparing work, always go back to the *beginning* of the project; this will help reduce subtle changes over time.

Most importantly, *have fun*! The old adage of "if you do what you love you will never work another day in your life" is very true. Every once in a while, step back from the project and look at what you have done and what you are going to do, remembering that what you do will help future researchers create new bodies of knowledge as well as nonresearchers experience things that they would not normally ever see, with your project serving as a window to other lifestyles, the past, and at times the future; this is why we do projects like this.

CHECKLIST FOR CHAPTER 7 — FINISHING UP

1. Do you have the means to properly store the original source material? Record albums, cassettes, videotapes and discs all have different, albeit similar, storage requirements. Heat and moisture are the enemies of all these sources.
2. Where and how will the data be stored? If using a commercial vendor or site, what are their retention policies. What about security and privacy.

If done locally, do you have the resources to manage the data over a long period of time.

3. What taxonomies or metadata structures will be used. Depending on the structure used, will it work with any discovery tools you have or will the data reside separately in its own finding aid, thereby making it less accessible to the casual researcher.

4. Do you have provisions for documenting and updating information on the project. This can be important if there are multiple people working on the project or if someone should leave the project and new personnel have to be brought in.

5. Remember to create "landmarks" so that you can see the forward movement of a project. Celebrate them as it will help keep everyone motivated and enthusiastic about the project.

Glossary

This is a selected glossary of terms used in this book. As such, they are *topic specific* in that they are used in the context of the information and subject matter of this book.

AC Air conditioning
A term typically used to describe the cooling of air for a room via mechanical means.

AAC Advanced Audio Coding
A **lossy** audio format designed to replace MP3. Generally should be avoided for archival work.

Acoustic Feet or Acoustic Isolator
A device that helps to isolate the source placed on it from surface vibrations.

ADC Converter
A device that converts an analog audio or video signal to a digital format.

Amplifier
A device that is used to boost the level of an audio signal so it can be used to drive **speakers** to a listening level or from one source to another so it can be utilized.

Anti-Skating
The process of canceling or offsetting a needle's natural tendency to want to move toward the center of the album. Anti-skating is a force applied to the tone arm to counteract this. It "pulls" the arm outward in an amount equal to cancel out the inward force; this keeps the stylus in the center of the groove and with equal wear on both sides of the stylus and groove.

Audiophile
One who has developed one's ear and/or has an affinity for music. It is not so much a love for music but knowing what to listen for in an audio environment to evaluate equipment and the quality of reproduced sound.

Authoring
The process of editing a file into the final form. It does *not* actually generate the final product. That process is called **mastering**.

Automatic Turntable
A **turntable** where the unit will place the **stylus** at the beginning of the record and automatically remove and replace it at the end of a record.

Beta Betamax
A home video system developed by the Sony Corporation. It utilized the same format at the **U-matic** system, but in a consumer environment that utilized a ½ in. tape in a cassette shell.

Big-Box Store
Term used to describe a store that is physically large and sells a variety of products, typically not focusing on a specific market or area of expertise.

Broadcast Quality
A recording made on equipment of high enough quality to be used on either broadcast or cable video stations or when used for audio, to be considered of high enough quality to be acceptable for commercial distribution.

Cartridge
The part of a **turntable** that is at the end of the **tonearm** that holds the stylus, or needle.

Cassette
Either the shell used to contain video tape or the commercial sound product introduced by the Philips Corporation.

CD Compact Disc
A digital disc format developed by the Philips Corporation, primarily to play music, but can also be used to store data.

Chromium Dioxide (CrO_2)
A tape formulation that allows for a higher recording level, designed to overcome tape hiss.

Coax
Short for *Coaxial Cable*. Typically, this is a "cable" where the center wire is wrapped by insulation, then surrounded by a braided string of wires which are ultimately surrounded by a coating. It is typically found in older television and video applications.

Color Correction
The process of "correcting" the color on a stored image so it is "correct." This could be if the original image has faded or turned to **sepia** when the original image is in black and white. It should *never* be used on the master image, only on distribution images.

Color Falsing
Essentially the same as **color correction**. Where the editor or operator changes the image to make it "correct" when the original image has degraded or suffered damage.

Compression
The process of making a file smaller so that it takes up less storage space. Some methods are **lossy** meaning that you will lose data and end up with a degraded output. MP3 and MPEG are examples of lossy formats.

Counterweight

The weight on a **tonearm** on the opposite end of the **head shell** that is used to balance and adjust the **tracking force** of the **stylus**.

Cropping

The process of "cutting off" the edges of an image, either still or video. It is frequently used as an editing tool, but is undesirable when capturing an image and the camera or scanner "crops" or cuts off part of the edge(s) of an image.

CRT Cathode Ray Tube

Technology used in first-generation televisions and computer monitors. They typically are large and bulky, but can provide a high degree of picture accuracy.

Cueing

The method whereby the tone arm is lowered to the record surface.

Demagnetizer

A device used to remove the residual magnetic build up from a tape head.

DIN Connector

A connector standardized by the *Deutsches Institut für Normung*. It is typically used for audio connections.

Disc

An *optically* based data storage format. It is not affected by magnetic fields and can be used to store sound or video in an analog or digital format.

Discovery Tool

A computer program that serves as an interface to multiple resources. It typically "crawls" the resources available and presents them in a single search interface.

Discrete

A process where each channel or signal in a recording and storage process has its own storage space. Stereo has two discrete channels, and Dolby 5.1 found in many home theater applications has six discrete channels.

Discwasher®

Commercial name for a dedicated cleaning system for records. Now made by the RCA Corporation.

Disk

A *magnetic* data storage format that can be used to store either sound or video in a digital format.

DJ Disc Jockey

Originally, a person who played records at a radio station, but now it is typically used to describe a person who plays music, often on albums but not necessarily, for performances and recordings.

Dolby-B

An **equalization** process designed to overcome the effects of tape hiss on audio cassettes.

DPI Dots Per Inch
A measure of the detail or resolution of a scanned image. As a general rule, the more dots per inch the better.

DVD Digital Versatile/Video Disc
A digital format used to store video images. Technically, "DVD" doesn't stand for anything but is generally understood to mean either **Digital Video Disc** or **Digital Versatile Disc** since the format can also be used to store music and/or data.

8 Track
A tape format popular in the 70s and 80s. It used a continuous loop of tape inside a sealed container. It was prone to failure due to the frictions the tape was subjected to and could not be rewound, only fast-forwarded.

ELP Extended Long Play
The slowest speed found on a **VCR**. It is typically not found on most home units. It can yield up to eight hours of recording time, but with a significant reduction in quality from other speeds.

Equalization
The process of modifying recorded sound to either overcome deficiencies in the equipment or listening area, or to modify the sound to create a "sound" that is different from that of the original to satisfy a target audience.

EXIF Exchangeable Image File Format
An industry standard that writes specific pieces of information about a capture device, typically a camera, to a file that is retained along with the image. It can be viewed either via dedicated viewer or by standard tools in the Windows operating system.

Falsing
See **Color Falsing.**

Ferro Chrome (FrCr)
A tape formulation that allowed for a higher input recording level; designed to help reduce tape hiss.

Fluorescent Lighting
A lighting source that uses electricity to excite a gas in a tube. It is most effective in long-term applications and is highly energy efficient and can be designed for different lighting applications but can generate an audible 60Hz hum.

Flutter
Short speed variations that can impact the upper frequencies of records.

GB Gigabyte
In computer terminology, 1,000,000,000 bytes or pieces of data.

Halogen Lighting
Similar to an **incandescent** light, other gasses are added that permit the light to operate hotter, and therefor brighter, than an incandescent lamp. They typically generate large quantities of heat and must be handled and used with great care.

Head Amplifier

A dedicated amplifier used to boost the output from a **turntable** to that which can be used by the tape inputs on a **receiver**.

Head Shell

The assembly at the end of a **tone arm** that holds the **cartridge**.

Headphones

Essentially speakers that sit on or over the ears. Like speakers, they come in many different styles and price points, with corresponding levels of quality and sound reproduction accuracy.

Hunt Lines

Scratches or lines on a record label caused by a **spindle** when placing a record on a **turntable** and the hold on the record is not aligned exactly with the **spindle**.

HVAC Heating, Ventilation, and Air Conditioning

A term used to describe the science and technology of processing and circulating the air in a given environment. It can include, but is not limited to, heating the air, cooling the air, circulating the air in a room, filtering that air, and making the air damper or drier, depending on the ambient environment and the needs of the room.

Incandescent Lighting

Light source that depends on the heating and glowing of a filament. It typically generates a large volume of heat. It is represented by the format most people think of when they think of a "light bulb."

Jacket

The cardboard external container used to hold a record or an album.

JPEG Joint Photographers Expert Group

A method of storing digital images. It is quite common, but is frequently a lossy format and does not lend itself readily to multiple images being combined into a single file.

Keystoning

A phenomenon whereby the top of an image is larger than the bottom of an image, so called because it mimics the shape of a keystone in an arch. It is typically caused by an off-center scan or photograph of an image.

Laserdisc

A proprietary video format developed by the Pioneer Corporation. It uses a laser beam to read analog video and digital signals. It is a loss-less technology superior to **VHS** and **Beta** tape formats.

LCD Liquid Crystal Display

A technology that uses liquid crystals to modify the light from a source to generate a video image. They *do not* generate light themselves, but turn themselves "on and off" to allow certain spectrums of light to pass.

LCNAF

The **Library of Congress Name Authority File** is a file, similar to **LCSH** that contains the "authorized" forms of personal and corporate names as well as uniform titles used in the United States.

LCSH Library of Congress Subject Headings
A controlled vocabulary of terms used to describe what an item or image is about. It is maintained by the Library of Congress but includes contributions by other approved libraries around the United States.

LED Light-Emitting Diode
A semiconductor-based light source that does not depend on a glowing filament to generate light. It is typically a "cool" light source in that it does not generate much heat nor consume a large quantity of electricity.

Light Box
Also known as a **light table**, it is a surface on which slide can be placed with a neutral light source behind them to be viewed.

Line-Level
An industry standard electrical level for passing analog signals between devices.

LP Long Play
A speed that is slower than **standard play** on a **VCR**. It will usually yield four hours of recording time, but at reduced quality from standard play.

Loss-Less
A data compression format that does not result in the loss of any data.

Lossy
A concept whereby during the process of manipulating or saving an audio or visual source, some of the original information is discarded to save space. Generally not indicated for use in an archival environment.

Loupe
A small magnification device typically used to enlarge detail on a viewed image. The lenses are usually enclosed in some type of cylinder or base.

Manual Turntable
A **turntable** where the user has to place the **stylus** at the beginning of the record and manually remove it at the end.

MARC
Machine readable cataloging standard developed by the Library of Congress to facilitate cataloging record interchange during the 60s. Scheduled to be replaced by a new data structure sometime in 2015–2018.

Master File
The original file generated when transcribing a source. It is unedited and in the same quality with no enhancements or clean-ups from the original source.

Mastering
The process of taking a final, edited product and actually placing it on a carrier, be it a CD, DVD, or other carrier.

Metadata
Essentially "data about data." It is often a group of terms or data links that are used to describe what an image or recording is about, where it was made, the format it is in, and so on.

Micro-Groove

A recording system developed in the 40s that permitted more groove to be placed on a record surface, thereby increasing the playing time.

Mirror Site

The process whereby a database or service is hosted on multiple sites around the world or in a country. Designed to improve system performance and response time.

NACO

The **Name Authority Cooperative** is a process whereby a library or organization can, after training and quality checks, contribute records to the **LCNAF** with the same authority as the Library of Congress.

NTSC National Television System Committee

The analog video standard used in most of the Americas and some Asian countries.

OLAC

The **Online Audio-Visual Catalogers** organization, which is devoted to the study and improvement of non-book cataloging. Can be found at www.olacinc.org.

Onionskin

A type of paper frequently used in better-quality record sleeves. Preferable to standard paper sleeves and plastic sleeves.

OPAC

The **online public access catalog** for many years was the public interface to the library's catalog. This role has been supplanted in many libraries by **discovery tools**.

OS Operating System

The set of instructions that help a computer to function, or "operate." Some common operating systems are Windows, Apple, and Unix.

Parallax Error

Errors introduced into the visual capture of an image because the source (e.g., a picture) is not directly aligned with the capture device (e.g., a camera.) Oftentimes it can be "corrected" with visual editing software.

Phono

Short for *phonograph*. It is used either as a term to describe a turntable or the cable/plug whereby a turntable is connected to another device.

Pinch Roller

A rubber wheel, typically in a cassette deck, that is used to control the speed of the tape past the record/playback head.

Platter

That part of a **turntable** that rotates, thereby turning the record.

Quartz-Locked

A technology that uses a quartz oscillator to keep the rotation of a turntable platter constant. It is more accurate than depending on the line frequency to determine accurate platter rotation.

RAM Random Access Memory
That part of computer memory that is most dynamic and also the fastest. As a general rule, it has the lowest access time but is typically lost when the computer is turned off.

RCA Connector
An audio or video connector that has a central plug surrounded by an outer metal shield. It can be used for either analog or digital formats, but is most typically found in the analog environment.

Receiver
Also known as a stereo receiver. It typically permits the input of multiple audio and video sources that can be individually selected and possibly manipulated. It also contains **amplifiers**, which boost the signal loud enough so that it can be used to drive speakers.

Reel-to-Reel
A tape format, either audio or video, where the tape is on exposed reels that are placed on the spindles of a player and threaded past the recording heads. In most applications, this structure yields the highest sound and picture quality.

Resonance
A condition where an input device picks up the vibrations from its own amplified output signal through a surface or vibrations and starts vibrating on its own, typically at low frequencies and causing a "hum" or buzz in the recording.

RIAA Equalization Curve
An **equalization** standard developed in the 30s and 40s and ultimately standardized in the 50s to compensate for the limitations of record albums and other analog disc-based recording formats.

Ripping
The process of taking a CD or DVD source and "breaking it down" so the contents can be edited or modified. When done with commercial recordings is often illegal.

RPM Revolutions per Minute
Used in conjunction to describe how fast a disc turns when playing audio or video signals. For record albums, the most common speeds are 78, 45, 33⅓, and 16 rpm.

S-Connector
A connection and cabling method developed in the 90s. It permits higher signal quality transfer for video images than standard **RCA** cables.

Semi-Automatic Turntable
A **turntable** where the user has to place the **stylus** manually at the beginning of a record, but the **turntable** will lift and replace it at the end of the record.

Sepia Tones
The pinkish-tinted color one frequently finds on older photographs or films. It is caused by a breakdown in the pigments in the original image.

Scanner
A device designed to convert some type of visual image (e.g., a photograph or map or letter) into a digital format that a computer can manipulate.

SelectaVision
A video disc format developed by the RCA Corporation to compete against **laser-discs**. It used a need in a needle-in-a-groove format similar to a record album. It did not find wide acceptance in the consumer market.

Shrink-Wrap
Thin, clear plastic that is applied hot to a product so that it "shrinks" as it cools, thereby sealing the product inside. It should be removed when found on record albums as it can hold dust and the wrap can cause the record to warp.

16 mm 16 millimeter
A standard commercial film width used in schools and other educational environments. It describes the width of the film in millimeters, as opposed to 8mm for home use and 35mm for many theater applications.

60 Hz
60 Hertz. The frequency that electricity cycles each second in the United States.

Sleeve
A paper or onion skin wrapper or holder that an album is inserted into before it is placed back in the **jacket**.

Son-Father-Grandfather
A process that uses three rotating backups. The first is the son. The next one made becomes the new "son" and the first "son" becomes the "father." The third "son" then makes the second "son" the "father" and the first "son" becomes the "grandfather." This process is rotated among all three backups.

SP Standard Play
The "base" speed on most **VCR**s. It will typically yield a two-hour recording time and the highest quality.

Speakers
Devices that convert audio signals into sound waves. They come in many different sizes and styles. Regardless of their design, every speaker involves tradeoffs in terms of price, sound, and size.

Spindle
The post in the middle of **platter** that the record fits over.

Strobe Light
A light that blinks on and off, sometimes very quickly. On **turntables**, a strobe light that turns on and off 60 times a second is often placed along the edge of the **platter** so that a corresponding row of dots can be used to verify the correct speed of the platter.

Stylus
In a turntable, that part of the **cartridge** that is actually the needle. Typically, it can be replaced independent of the cartridge on most audiophile-level systems.

Stylus Force Gauge
An external device used to accurately measure the **tracking force** of a **cartridge/** stylus.

SLP Super Long Play
A slower recording speed on **VCR**s that will usually yield six hours of recording on a standard cassette, but at significantly reduced quality.

TB Terabyte
A computer term used to designate 1,000,000,000,000 bytes of data, or 1,000 GB.

35 mm 35 millimeter
The standard size for professional and most higher-quality film photographic work.

TIFF Tagged Image File Format
A loss-less format frequently used to store images. Its greatest strength is that multiple images can easily be scanned and stored in a single file.

Tonearm
That part of a **turntable** that holds the **cartridge**.

Trackball
A computer pointing device, similar to a mouse, except that it typically uses a large ball to control the screen pointer. While designs vary, it is really nothing more than a standard mouse turned upside down. It is a device often preferred by gamers due to its high level of speed and less demanding space requirements.

Tracking
In early **VCR**s, the tracking adjustment was a manual adjustment that could be made to adjust how the tape passed over the record/play head to optimize the signal. This adjustment is now performed automatically by newer VCRs.

Tracking Force
This is the downward force that a stylus presses down on a record album with. It is **cartridge** and **stylus** specific and is specified by the manufacturer.

Turntable
Colloquially known as a record player, this device is used to play record albums, singles, and other "flat" analog recorded material. The basic parts of a turntable are **tonearm**, **platter,** and **cartridge**.

U-Matic
A modified version of Sony's reel-to-reel video recording system. It differs from the commercial version in that the tape is contained in a cassette shell rather than open.

Upconversion
The process of taking a video signal and increasing the resolution of the signal so that it has more scanning lines. Technically, it does not "improve" the signal, but creates the illusion of a better image since more scan lines are used. Frequently done by Blu-ray **DVD** players and some receivers.

UPS Uninterruptable Power Supply
A device that the power cord of a computer plugs into to ensure a limited supply of electricity to a computer (and other connected peripherals) when the main power goes down or becomes unstable. It is designed to enable a "controlled shutdown" of a computer whereby you can save any items you are currently working on.

USB Universal Serial Bus
A cable and connector standard developed in the mid-1990s by the computer industry to connect peripherals to a computer.

USB Hub
A device that connects to a **USB** port on computer to give you more USB connections. Similar in operation to what a strip outlet does for electrical outlets.

VCR Videocassette Recorder
A device used to record signals from a broadcast or other external source, typically onto a cassette. The most common formats are **VHS**, **Beta,** and **U-matic**. Some units will only play back a tape; these are typically called videocassette players.

VHS Video Home System
A home video recording system developed by the Victor Company of Japan (JVC), which utilized a ½ in. tape format in a helical scanning format.

VIAF Virtual Internet Authority File
A program hosted by OCLC Inc. that combines multiple national authority files and creates linkages to similar name terms.

Video Rot
A problem in first-generation and inexpensive **laserdiscs** that would cause the disc surface to de-laminate from the substrate, rendering the disc unplayable.

WAV Files
The **waveform audio file format** is a Microsoft and IBM audio file format used for storing an audio bitstream on PCs. It is a lossless format.

WinZip
A proprietary file compression process. It is lossless but not the most efficient format to use for audio and video files.

Wow
A slow change in the rotation speed of the turntable that can alter the lowest notes on a record.

Index

About the Author

SCOTT PIEPENBURG is currently Head of Cataloging at Valdosta State University in Valdosta, Georgia. His prior experience includes the position of cataloging coordinator at the University of Wisconsin–Stevens Point and district cataloger/system administrator for the Dallas Independent School District where he was instrumental in bringing up the initial DALLINK project, the first large-urban union catalog in the United States. His work experience includes work at Hampton University, a HBCU in Virginia as well as Vincennes University in Indiana. Not limited to only working in libraries, he has worked at such vendors as EBSCO, Infotrieve, and Follett Software, being one of the developers of the original Alliance+ product and the Unison software product, which served as the basis for the current Destiny product.

Scott is the author of the popular *Easy MARC* series as well as articles on the future of library automation, the history of disc-based recording technology, and the role of cataloging AV materials for school and public libraries. He has lectured around the United States on the topics of cataloging in general and authority control in particular and considers himself an "authority control junkie." He is currently working on a transition guide from AACR2 to RDA as well as editing a book on digital archives. His other library-related interests include net neutrality where he is working on an article for *The Objective Standard* as well as the role of Objectivism in library collection development and digitization costs and archival concerns.